PARALLEL AND DISTRIBUTED INFORMATION SYSTEMS

edited by

Jeffrey F. Naughton
University of Wisconsin-Madison

Gerhard Weikum
University of the Saarland

A Special Issue of
DISTRIBUTED AND PARALLEL DATABASES
An International Journal
Volume 6, No. 1 (1998)

KLUWER ACADEMIC PUBLISHERS
Boston / Dordrecht / London

DISTRIBUTED AND PARALLEL DATABASES

Volume 6, No. 1, January 1998

Special Issue on Parallel and Distributed Information Systems

Guest Editors: Jeffrey F. Naughton and Gerhard Weikum

Distributors for North America:
Kluwer Academic Publishers
101 Philip Drive
Assinippi Park
Norwell, Massachusetts 02061 USA

Distributors for all other countries:
Kluwer Academic Publishers Group
Distribution Centre
Post Office Box 322
3300 AH Dordrecht, THE NETHERLANDS
e-ISBN

ISBN 978-1-4419-5026-0

Library of Congress Cataloging-in-Publication Data

A C.I.P. Catalogue record for this book is available
from the Library of Congress.

Printed on acid-free paper.

Distributed and Parallel Databases, 6, 5–6 (1998)

Guest Editors' Introduction

This special issue contains extended versions of three contributions that have been selected as the best papers of the 4th International Conference on Parallel and Distributed Information Systems (PDIS'96), which was held in Miami Beach in December 1996. Parallel and distributed database technology is at the heart of many mission-critical applications such as online transaction processing, data warehousing, business workflow management, interoperable information systems, and information brokering in global networks. While commercial systems in this arena are gradually maturing, new challenges are posed by the growing demand for large-scale, enterprise-wide solutions and the proliferation of services on the information superhighway. Future parallel and distributed information systems will have to support millions of clients and will face tremendous scalability challenges with regard to massive data volume, performance, availability, and also administration and long-term maintenance.

The three selected papers reflect these trends and cover a good fraction of the challenging issues. The first paper, by Yue Zhuge, Hector Garcia-Molina, and Janet Wiener, investigates the incremental maintenance of materialized select-project-join views in a data warehouse. More specifically, it addresses the problem that additional queries against the data sources that are necessary for the view maintenance may interfere with concurrent updates on the sources. The paper develops a family of view maintenance algorithms, coined the Strobe algorithms, that guarantee consistency of the view while allowing transactions of different complexity levels on the data sources. In addition to developing these fully implemented, practically useful algorithms, the paper also provides insight into the fundamental tradeoffs in keeping warehouse data consistent with data sources, an issue that is likely to gain importance as more and more mission-critical applications will be based on data warehousing technology.

The second paper, by Rajeev Rastogi, Philip Bohannon, James Parker, Avi Silberschatz, S. Seshadri, and S. Sudarshan, considers very-high-throughput applications that pose extremely stringent requirements on transaction response time, often on the order of milliseconds, for example, for call routing and switching in telecommunications. To meet these demands, the paper pursues a parallel, main-memory database system with shared disks but distributed memory. For this setting, a new multi-level recovery method is developed with low logging overhead, fast restart, and, ultimately, very high system availability. With rapidly decreasing RAM prices on the one hand, and the very high performance and availability requirements on the other, this work can be expected to be relevant beyond its initial targets in the telecommunications area.

The third paper, by Yannis Papakonstantinou, Ashish Gupta, and Laura Haas, aims at providing integrated access to widely heterogeneous information sources, one of the most challenging problems posed on the information superhighway. The paper's approach is based on a mediator architecture, where the mediator translates global queries into sub-queries that can be executed on the various data sources. In contrast to prior work that wraps each source with a lowest-common-denominator functionality, the novel aspect here is that the mediator is made aware of the sources' querying capabilities and exploits them to the best possible extent. The paper develops both a framework for describing the sources' capabilities and an effective and efficient query rewriting algorithm.

The three articles in this issue have been selected by the program committee of the PDIS'96 conference. We solicited extended versions from the authors to archive their research contributions in a widely read journal. The extended papers have again been reviewed, and we believe that their quality is indeed outstanding. We hope that the readers will find these papers as innovative and insightful as we did.

Jeff Naughton and Gerhard Weikum
PDIS'96 Program Committee Co-chairs

Distributed and Parallel Databases, 6, 7–40 (1998)
© 1998 Kluwer Academic Publishers.

Consistency Algorithms for Multi-Source Warehouse View Maintenance * **

YUE ZHUGE   zhuge@cs.stanford.edu

HECTOR GARCIA-MOLINA   hector@cs.stanford.edu

JANET L. WIENER   wiener@cs.stanford.edu
Computer Science Department, Stanford University, Stanford, CA 94305

Recommended by: Jeffrey F. Naughton and Gerhard Weikum

Abstract. A warehouse is a data repository containing integrated information for efficient querying and analysis. Maintaining the consistency of warehouse data is challenging, especially if the data sources are autonomous and views of the data at the warehouse span multiple sources. Transactions containing multiple updates at one or more sources, e.g., batch updates, complicate the consistency problem. In this paper we identify and discuss three fundamental transaction processing scenarios for data warehousing. We define four levels of consistency for warehouse data and present a new family of algorithms, the Strobe family, that maintain consistency as the warehouse is updated, under the various warehousing scenarios. All of the algorithms are incremental and can handle a continuous and overlapping stream of updates from the sources. Our implementation shows that the algorithms are practical and realistic choices for a wide variety of update scenarios.

Keywords: data warehouse, data integration, data consistency, materialized view maintenance

1. Introduction

A *data warehouse* is a repository of integrated information from distributed, autonomous, and possibly heterogeneous, sources. Figure 1 illustrates the basic warehouse architecture. At each source, a monitor collects the data of interest and sends it to the warehouse. The monitors are responsible for identifying changes in the source data, and notifying the warehouse. If a source provides relational-style triggers, the monitor may simply pass on information. On the other hand, a monitor for a legacy source may need to compute the difference between successive snapshots of the source data. At the warehouse, the integrator receives the source data, performs any necessary data integration or translation, adds any extra desired information, such as timestamps for historical analysis, and tells the warehouse to store the data. In effect, the warehouse caches a materialized view of the source data. The data is then readily available to user applications for querying and analysis.

Most current commercial warehousing systems (e.g., Prism, Redbrick) focus on storing the data for efficient access, and on providing extensive querying facilities at the warehouse.

* This work was partially supported by Rome Laboratories under Air Force Contract F30602-94-C-0237; by an equipment grant from Digital Equipment Corporation; and by the Advanced Research and Development Committee of the Community Management Staff, as a project in the Massive Digital Data Systems Program.
** This paper is an extended version of a paper published in International Conference on Parallel and Distributed Information Systems, December 1996. The main additions are in Section 6.2 and Section 8. Also, we included the full proof of correctness of Strobe and C-Strobe algorithm in Appendix A. Proof of Correctness for Strobe Algorithm and B. Proof of Correctness for Complete Strobe Algorithm.

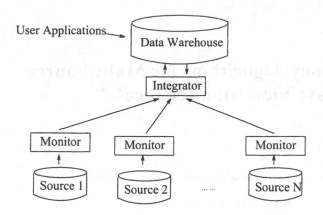

Figure 1. Data warehouse architecture

They ignore the complementary problem of consistently integrating new data, assuming that this happens "off line," while queries are not being run. Of course, they are discovering that many customers have international operations in multiple time zones, so there is no convenient down time, a "night" or "weekend" when all of the recent updates can be batched and processed together, and materialized views can be recomputed. Furthermore, as more and more updates occur, the down time window may no longer be sufficient to process all of the updates [10].

Thus, there is substantial interest in warehouses that can absorb incoming updates and incrementally modify the materialized views at the warehouse, without halting query processing. In this paper we focus on this process and on how to ensure that queries see consistent data. The crux of the problem is that each arriving update may need to be integrated with data from other sources before being stored at the warehouse. During this processing, more updates may arrive at the warehouse, causing the warehouse to become inconsistent.

The following example illustrates some of the inconsistencies that may arise. For simplicity, we assume that both the warehouse and the sources use the relational model, and that the materialized view kept at the warehouse contains the key for each participating relation. In this example, each update is a separate transaction at one of the sources.

EXAMPLE 1:   View updating anomaly over multiple sources

Let view V be defined as $V = r_1 \bowtie r_2 \bowtie r_3$, where r_1, r_2, r_3 are three relations residing on sources x, y and z, respectively. Initially, the relations are

$$r_1 : \begin{array}{cc} A & B \\ \hline 1 & 2 \end{array} \qquad r_2 : \begin{array}{cc} B & C \\ \hline - & - \end{array} \qquad r_3 : \begin{array}{cc} C & D \\ \hline 3 & 4 \end{array}$$

The materialized view at the warehouse is $MV = \emptyset$. We consider two source updates: $U_1 = insert(r_2, [2, 3])$ and $U_2 = delete(r_1, [1, 2])$. Using a conventional incremental view maintenance algorithm [5], the following events may occur at the warehouse.

1. The warehouse receives $U_1 = insert(r_2, [2, 3])$ from source y. It generates query $Q_1 = r_1 \bowtie [2, 3] \bowtie r_3$. To evaluate Q_1, the warehouse first sends query $Q_1^1 = r_1 \bowtie [2, 3]$ to source x.

2. The warehouse receives $A_1^1 = [1, 2, 3]$ from source x. Query $Q_1^2 = [1, 2, 3] \bowtie r_3$ is sent to source z for evaluation.

3. The warehouse receives $U_2 = delete(r_1, [1, 2])$ from source x. Since the current view is empty, no action is taken for this deletion.

4. The warehouse receives $A_1^2 = [1, 2, 3, 4]$ from source z, which is the final answer for Q_1. Since there are no pending queries or updates, the answer is inserted into MV and $MV = [1, 2, 3, 4]$. This final view is incorrect. $\qquad\square$

In this example, the interleaving of query Q_1 with updates arriving from the sources causes the incorrect view. Note that even if the warehouse view is updated by completely recomputing the view — an approach taken by several commercial systems, such as Bull and Pyramid — the warehouse is subject to the same anomalies caused by the interleaving of updates with recomputation.

There are two straightforward ways to avoid this type of inconsistency, but we will argue that in general, neither one is desirable. The first way is to is store copies of all relations at the warehouse. In our example, Q_1 could then be atomically evaluated at the warehouse, causing tuple $[1, 2, 3, 4]$ to be added to MV. When U_2 arrives, the tuple is deleted from MV, yielding a correct final warehouse state. While this solution may be adequate for some applications, we believe it has several disadvantages. First, the storage requirement at the warehouse may be very high. For instance, suppose that r_3 contains data on companies, e.g., their name, stock price, and profit history. If we copy all of r_3 at the warehouse, we need to keep tuples for *all* companies that exist anywhere in the world, not just those we are currently interested in tracking. (If we do not keep data for all companies, in the future we may not be able to answer a query that refers to a new company, or a company we did not previously track, and be unable to atomically update the warehouse.) Second, the warehouse must integrate updates for all of the source data, not just the data of interest. In our company example, we would need to update the stock prices of all companies, as the prices change. This can represent a very high update load [6], much of it to data we may never need. Third, due to cost, copyright or security, storing copies of all of the source data may not be feasible. For example, the source access charges may be proportional to the amount of data we track at the warehouse.

The second straightforward way to avoid inconsistencies is to run each update and all the actions needed to incrementally integrate it into the warehouse as a distributed transaction spanning the warehouse and all the sources involved. In our example, if Q_1 runs as part of a distributed transaction, then it can read a consistent snapshot and properly update the warehouse. However, distributed transactions require a global concurrency control mechanism spanning all the sources, which may not exist. And even if it does, the sources may be unwilling to tolerate the delays that come with global concurrency control.

Instead, our approach is to make queries *appear* atomic by processing them intelligently at the warehouse (and without requiring warehouse copies of all relations). In our example, the warehouse notes that deletion U_2 arrived at the warehouse while it was processing query

Q_1. Therefore, answer A_1 may contain some tuples that reflect the deleted r_1 tuple. Indeed, A_1 contains $[1, 2, 3, 4]$ which should not exist after $[1, 2]$ was deleted from r_1. Thus, the warehouse removes this tuple, leaving an empty answer. The materialized view is then left empty, which is the correct state after both updates take place. The above example gives the "flavor" of our solution; we will present more details as we explain our algorithms.

Note that the intelligent processing of updates at the warehouse depends on how and if sources run transactions. If some sources run transactions, then we need to treat their updates, whether they came from one source or multiple sources, as atomic units. Combining updates into atomic warehouse actions introduces additional complexities that will be handled by our algorithms. Since we do not wish to assume a particular transaction scenario, in this paper we cover the three main possibilities: sources run no transactions, some sources run local (but not global) transactions, and some sources run global transactions.

Although we are fairly broad in the transaction scenarios we consider, we do make two key simplifying assumptions: we assume that warehouse views are defined by relational project, select, join (PSJ) operations, and we assume that these views include the keys of all of the relations involved. We believe that PSJ views are the most common and therefore, it is a good subproblem on which to focus initially. We believe that requiring keys is a reasonable assumption, since keys make it easier for the applications to interpret and handle the warehouse data. Furthermore, if a user-specified view does not contain sufficient key information, the warehouse can simply add the key attributes to the view definition. (We have developed view maintenance algorithms for the case where some key data is not present, but they are not discussed here. They are substantially more complex than the ones presented here — another reason for including keys in the view.)

In our previous work [28] we considered a very restricted scenario: all warehouse data arrived from a single source. Even in that simple case, there are consistency problems, and we developed algorithms for solving them. However, in the more realistic multi-source scenario, it becomes *significantly* more complex to maintain consistent views. (For instance, the ECA and ECA-Key algorithms of [28] do not provide consistency in Example 1; they lead to the same incorrect execution shown.) In particular, the complexities not covered in our earlier work are as follows.

- An update from one source may need to be integrated with data from several other sources. However, gathering the data corresponding to one view update is not an atomic operation. No matter how fast the warehouse generates the appropriate query and sends it to the sources, receiving the answer is not atomic, because parts of it come from different, autonomous sources. Nonetheless, the view should be updated as if all of the sources were queried atomically.

- Individual sources may batch several updates into a single, source-local, transaction. For example, the warehouse may receive an entire day's updates in one transaction. These updates — after integration with data from other sources — should appear atomically at the warehouse. Furthermore, updates from several sources may together comprise one, global, transaction, which again must be handled atomically.

These complexities lead to substantially different solutions. In particular, the main contributions of this paper are:

1. We define and discuss all of the above update and transaction scenarios, which require increasingly complex algorithms.

2. We identify four levels of consistency for warehouse views defined on multiple sources, in increasing order of difficulty to guarantee. Note that as concurrent query and update processing at warehouses becomes more common, and as warehouse applications grow beyond "statistical analysis," there will be more concern from users about the consistency of the data they are accessing [10]. Thus, we believe it is important to offer customers a variety of consistency options and ways to enforce them.

3. We develop the Strobe family of algorithms to provide consistency for each of the transaction scenarios. We have implemented each of the Strobe algorithms in our warehouse prototype [26], demonstrating that the algorithms are practical and efficient.

4. We map out the space of warehouse maintenance algorithms (Figure 3). The algorithms we present in this paper provide a wide number of options for this consistency and distribution space.

The remainder of the paper is organized as follows. We discuss related work in Section 2. In Section 3, we define the three transaction scenarios and specify our assumptions about the order of messages and events in a warehouse environment. In Section 4 we define four levels of consistency and correctness, and discuss when each might be desirable. Then we describe our new algorithms in Section 5 and 6. We also demonstrate the levels of consistency that each algorithm achieves for the different transaction scenarios. In Section 7, we adapt the algorithms so that the warehouse can reflect every update individually, and show that the algorithms will terminate. Section 8 gives a brief overview of the algorithm implementation status. We conclude in Section 9 by outlining optimizations to our algorithms and our future work.

2. Related research

The work we describe in this paper is closely related to research in three fields: data warehousing, data consistency and incremental maintenance of materialized views. We discuss each in turn.

Data warehouses are large repositories for analytical data, and have recently generated tremendous interest in industry. A general description of the data warehousing idea may be found in [18]. Companies such as Red Brick and Prism have built specialized data warehousing software, while almost all other database vendors, such as Sybase, Oracle and IBM, are targeting their existing products to data warehousing applications.

A warehouse holds a copy of the source data, so essentially we have a distributed database system with replicated data. A good overview of the mechanisms for managing replicated data may be found in [4]. However, because of the autonomy of the sources, traditional concurrency mechanisms are often not applicable [3]. A variety of concurrency control schemes have been suggested over the years for such environments (for example, [1, 27, 14]). They either provide weaker notions of consistency, or exploit the semantics of applications. The algorithms we present in this paper exploit the semantics of materialized view maintenance to obtain consistency without traditional distributed concurrency control. Furthermore, they offer a variety of consistency levels that are useful in the context of warehousing.

Many incremental view maintenance algorithms have been developed for centralized database systems [5, 12, 9, 16, 21, 23, 7] and a good overview of materialized views and their maintenance can be found in [11]. Most of these solutions assume that a single system controls all of the base relations and understands the views and hence can intelligently monitor activities and compute all of the information that is needed for updating the views. As we showed in Example 1, when a centralized algorithm is applied to the warehouse, the warehouse user may see inconsistent views of the source data. These inconsistent views arise regardless of whether the centralized algorithm computes changes using the old base relations, as in [5], or using the new base relations, as in [7]. The crux of the warehouse problem is that the exact state of the base relations (old or new) when the incremental changes are computed at the sources is unknown, and our algorithms filter out or add in recent modifications dynamically. Furthermore, all previous solutions require that the base relations be stable (e.g., locked) while computing the changes to the view. We allow modifications to the base relations to execute concurrently, and then compensate the proposed view changes for those modifications.

Previous distributed algorithms for view maintenance, such as those in [22, 24, 20], rely on timestamping the updated tuples. For a warehousing environment, sources can be legacy systems so we cannot assume that they will help by transmitting all necessary data or by attaching timestamps.

Hull and Zhou [17] provide a framework for supporting distributed data integration using materialized views. However, their approach first materializes each base relation (or relevant portion), then computes the view from the materialized copies. As a result, they emphasize finding out which copies of base relations need to be kept consistent and how, while we propose algorithms to maintain joined views directly, without storing any auxiliary data. We compare our definition of consistency with theirs in Section 4. Another recent paper by Baralis, et al. [2] also uses timestamps to maintain materialized views at a warehouse. However, they assume that the warehouse never needs to query the sources for more data, hence circumventing all of the consistency problems that we address.

A warehouse often processes updates (from one or more transactions) in batch mode. Conventional algorithms have no way to ensure that an entire transaction is reflected in the view at the same time, or that a batch representing an entire day (or hour, or week, or minute) of updates is propagated to the view simultaneously. In this paper we present view maintenance algorithms that address these problems.

Finally, as we mentioned in Section 1, in [28] we showed how to provide consistency in a restricted single-source environment. Here we study the more general case of multiple sources and transactions that may span sources.

3. Warehouse transaction environment

The complexity of designing consistent warehouse algorithms is closely related to the scope of transactions at the sources. The larger the scope of a transaction, the more complex the algorithm becomes. In this section, we define three common transaction scenarios, in increasing order of complexity, and spell out our assumptions about the warehouse environment. In particular, we address the ordering of messages between sources and the warehouse, and define a source *event*. We use the relational model for simplicity; each update therefore consists of a single tuple action such as inserting or deleting a tuple.

3.1. Update transaction scenarios

The three transaction scenarios we consider in this paper are:

1. *Single update transactions.* Single update transactions are the simplest; each update comprises its own transaction and is reported to the warehouse separately. Actions of legacy systems that do not have transactions fall in this category: as each change is detected by the source monitor, it is sent to the warehouse as a single update transaction.

2. *Source-local transactions.* A source-local transaction is a sequence of actions performed at the same source that together comprise one transaction. The goal is therefore to reflect all of these actions atomically at the warehouse. We assume that each source has a local serialization schedule of all of its source-local transactions. Single update transactions are special cases of source-local transactions. Database sources, for example, are likely to have source-local transactions. We also consider batches of updates that are reported together to be a single, source-local, transaction.

3. *Global transactions.* In this scenario there are global transactions that contain actions performed at multiple sources. We assume that there is a global serialization order of the global transactions. (If there is not, it does not matter how we order the transactions at the warehouse.) The goal is therefore to reflect the global transactions atomically at the warehouse. Depending on how much information the warehouse receives about the transaction, this goal is more or less achievable. For example, unless there are global transaction identifiers, or the entire transaction is reported by a single source, the warehouse cannot tell which source-local transactions together comprise a global transaction.

For each transaction scenario, we make slightly different assumptions about the contents of messages.

3.2. Messages

There are two types of messages from the sources to the warehouse: reporting an update and returning the answer to a query. There is only one type of message in the other direction; the warehouse may send queries to the sources.

We assume that each single update transaction and source-local transaction is reported in one message, at the time that the transaction commits. For example, a relational database source might trigger sending a message on transaction commit [25]. However, batching multiple transactions into the same message does not affect the algorithms of Section 5. For global transactions, updates can be delivered in a variety of ways. For example, the site that commits the transaction may collect all the updates and send them to the warehouse at the commit point. As an alternative, each site may send its own updates, once it knows the global transaction has committed. In Section 6.2 we discuss the implications of the different schemes.

3.3. Event Ordering

Each source action, plus the resulting message sent to the warehouse, is considered one event. For example, evaluating a query at a source and sending the answer back to the warehouse is considered one event. Events are atomic, and are ordered by the sequence of the corresponding actions.

We assume that any two messages sent from one source to the warehouse are delivered in the same order as they were sent. However, we place no restrictions on the order in which messages sent from different sources to the warehouse are delivered. That is, the sources are not coordinated. For example, even if a message from source x is sent prior to a message from source y, the warehouse may receive y's message first.

The second assumption (point-to-point message ordering) may not always hold, e.g., if two messages are sent by different routes; however, the crucial aspect is not that the messages arrive in order, but that they are processed in order. In our implementation, we add a sequence number to all messages sent by each source; the warehouse can then detect a missing message and wait for it before processing any later messages from that source.

The first assumption (atomic events at sources) is reasonable for sources that run transactions (either local or global), but may not be reasonable for legacy sources that have no transaction facilities. If such sources report their events in arbitrary order, then in some cases there is no way we can guarantee correctness. For example, if the source inserts a tuple and then deletes it, but report these events in reverse order, then there is no way for the warehouse to guess what actually happened. In other cases the warehouse may guarantee one of our weaker notions of consistency, for example, convergence. For ease of exposition we assume atomic events for all sources, and return to this issue in Section 9.

3.4. Discussion

In practice, the update transaction scenario seen at the warehouse depends primarily on the capabilities of the underlying sources. For example, it is currently common practice to report updates from a source periodically. Instead of reporting each change, a monitor might send all of the changes that occurred over the last hour or day to the warehouse, as a single batch transaction. Periodic snapshots may be the only way for the monitor of an unsophisticated legacy source to report changes, or a monitor might choose to report updates lazily when the warehouse does not need to be kept strictly up to date.

In general, smarter monitors (those which help to group or classify updates or those which coordinate global transactions) save the warehouse processing and may enable the warehouse to achieve a higher level of consistency, as we will see in Section 6.2. We believe that today most warehouse transaction environments will support either single-update transactions or source-local transactions (or both), but will not have any communication or coordination between sources. Still, for completeness, we believe it is important to understand the global transaction scenario, which may be more likely in the future.

4. Correctness and consistency

Before describing our algorithms, we first define what it means for an algorithm to be correct in an environment where activity at the sources is decoupled from the view at the warehouse. In particular, we are concerned with what it means for a warehouse view to be consistent with the original source data. Since each source update may involve fetching data from multiple sources in order to update the warehouse view, we first define *states* at the sources and at the warehouse.

4.1. Source and warehouse states

Each warehouse state ws represents the contents of the warehouse. The warehouse state changes whenever the view is updated. Let the warehouse states be $ws_0, ws_1, ws_2, \ldots, ws_f$. (We assume there is a final warehouse state after all activity ceases.) We consider one view V at the warehouse, which is defined over a set of base relations at one or more sources. The view at state ws_j is $V(ws_j)$.

Let there be u sources, where each source has a unique id x ($1 \leq x \leq u$). A source state ss is a vector that contains u elements and represents the (visible) state of each source at a given instant in time. The xth component, $ss[x]$, is the state of source x. Source states represent the contents of source base relations. We assume that source updates are executed is a serializable fashion across all sources, i.e., there is some serial schedule S that represents execution of the updates. (However, what constitutes a transaction varies according to the scenario.) We assume that ss_q is the final state after S completes. $V(ss)$ is the result of computing the view V over the source state ss. That is, for each relation r at source x that contributes to the view, $V(ss)$ is evaluated over r at the state $ss[x]$.

Each source transaction is guaranteed to bring the sources from one consistent state to another. For any serial schedule R, we use $result(R)$ to refer to the source state vector that results from its execution.

4.2. Levels of consistency

Assume that the view at the warehouse is initially synchronized with the source data, i.e., $V(ss_0) = V(ws_0)$. We define four levels of consistency for warehouse views. Each level subsumes all prior levels. These definition are a generalization of the ones in [28] for a multi-source warehouse environment.

1. **Convergence:** For all finite executions, $V(ws_f) = V(ss_q)$. That is, after the last update and after all activity has ceased, the view is consistent with the source data.

2. **Weak consistency:** Convergence holds and, for all ws_i, there exists a source state vector ss_j such that $V(ws_i) = V(ss_j)$. Furthermore, for each source x, there exists a serial schedule $R = T_1, \ldots, T_k$ of (a subset of all) transactions such that $result(R)[x] = ss_j[x]$. That is, each warehouse state reflects a valid state at each source, and there is a locally serializable schedule at each source that achieves that state. However, each source may reflect a different serializable schedule and the warehouse may reflect a different set of committed transactions at each source.

3. **Strong consistency:** Weak consistency holds and there exists a serial schedule R and a mapping m, from warehouse states into source states, with the following properties: (i) Serial schedule R is equivalent to the actual execution of transactions at the sources. It defines a sequence of source states $ss_1, ss_2, \ldots$ where ss_j reflects the first j transactions (i.e., $ss_j = result(R')$ where R' is the R prefix with j transactions). (ii) For all ws_i, $m(ws_i) = ss_j$ for some j and $V[ws_i] = V[ss_j]$. (iii) If $ws_i < ws_k$, then $m(ws_i) < m(ws_k)$. That is, each warehouse state reflects a set of valid source states, reflecting the *same* globally serializable schedule, and the order of the warehouse states matches the order of source actions.

4. **Completeness:** In addition to strong consistency, for every ss_j defined by R, there exists a ws_i such that $m(ws_i) = ss_j$. That is, there is a complete order-preserving mapping between the states of the view and the states of the sources.

Hull and Zhou's definition of consistency for replicated data [17] is similar to one of the levels we just defined: strong consistency, except that our strong consistency is less restrictive than theirs in that we do not require any fixed order between two non-conflicting actions. Our definition is compatible with standard serializability theory. In fact, our consistency definition can be rephrased in terms of serializability theory, by treating the warehouse view evaluation as a read only transaction [13] at the sources.

Although completeness is a nice property since it states that the view "tracks" the base data exactly, we believe it may be too strong a requirement and unnecessary in most practical warehousing scenarios. In some cases, convergence may be sufficient, i.e., knowing that "eventually" the warehouse will have a valid state, even if it passes through intermediate states that are invalid. In most cases, strong consistency is desirable, i.e., knowing that every warehouse state is valid with respect to a source state. In the next section, we show that an algorithm may achieve different levels of consistency depending on the update transaction scenario to which it is applied.

5. Strobe Algorithms

In the following three sections, we present the Strobe family of algorithms. The Strobe algorithms are named after strobe lights, because they periodically "freeze" the constantly changing sources into a consistent view at the warehouse. Each algorithm was designed to achieve a specific level of correctness for one of the three transaction processing scenarios. We discuss the algorithms in increasing level of complexity: the Strobe algorithm, which is the simplest, achieves strong consistency for single update transactions. The Transaction-Strobe algorithm achieves strong consistency for source-local transactions, and the Global-Strobe algorithm achieves strong consistency for global transactions. In Section 7 we present modifications to these algorithms that attain completeness for their respective transaction scenarios.

5.1. Terminology

First, we introduce the terminology that we use to describe the algorithms.

Definition 1. A view V at the warehouse over n relations is defined by a Project-Select-Join (PSJ) expression $V = \Pi_{proj}(\sigma_{cond}(r_1 \bowtie r_2 \bowtie \ldots \bowtie r_n))$.

Any two relations may reside at the same or at different sources, and any relational algebra expression constructed with project, select, and join operations can be transformed into an equivalent expression of this form. Moreover, although we describe our algorithms for PSJ views, our ideas can be used to adapt any existing centralized view maintenance algorithm to a warehousing environment.

As we mentioned in the introduction, we assume that the projection list contains the key attributes for each relation. We expect most applications to require keys anyway, and if not, they can be added to the view by the warehouse.

Definition 2. The materialized view MV of a view V is the current state of V at the warehouse, $V(ws)$.

When a view is defined over multiple sources, an update at one source is likely to initiate a multi-source query Q at the warehouse. Since we cannot assume that the sources will cooperate to answer Q, the warehouse must therefore decide where to send the query first.

Definition 3. Suppose we are given a query Q that needs to be evaluated. The function $next\_source(Q)$ returns the pair (x, Q^i) where x is the next source to contact, and Q^i is the portion of Q that can be evaluated at x. If Q does not need to be evaluated further, then x is *nil*. A^i is the answer received at the warehouse in response to subquery Q^i. Query $Q\langle A^i \rangle$ denotes the remaining query after answer A^i has been incorporated into query Q.

For PSJ queries, $next\_source$ will always choose a source containing a relation that can be joined with the known part of the query, rather than requiring the source to ship the entire base relation to the warehouse (which may not even be possible). As we will see later, queries generated by an algorithm can also be unions of PSJ expressions. For such queries, $next\_source$ simply selects one of the expressions for evaluation. An improvement would be to find common subexpressions.

EXAMPLE 2: Using $next\_source$

Let relations r_1, r_2, r_3 reside at sources x, y, z, respectively, let $V = r_1 \bowtie r_2 \bowtie r_3$, and let U_2 be an update to relation r_2 received at the warehouse. Therefore, query $Q = (r_1 \bowtie U_2 \bowtie r_3)$, and $next\_source(Q) = (x, Q^1 = r_1 \bowtie U_2)$. When the warehouse receives answer A^1 from x, $Q\langle A^1 \rangle = A^1 \bowtie r_3$. Then $next\_source(A^1 \bowtie r_3) = (z, Q^2 = A^1 \bowtie r_3)$, since there is only one relation left to join in the query. A^2 is the final answer. □

In the above example, the query was sent to source x first. Alternatively, $next\_source(Q) = (z, U_2 \bowtie r_3)$. When there is more than one possible relation to join with the intermediate result, $next\_source$ may use statistics (such as those used by query optimizers) to decide which part of the query to evaluate next.

We are now ready to define the procedure $source\_evaluate$, which loops to compute the next portion of query Q until the final result answer A is received. In the procedure, WQ is the "working query" portion of query Q, i.e., the part of Q that has not yet been evaluated.

$source\_evaluate(Q)$: returns answers to Q
1.   Begin
2.   i = 0; $WQ = Q$; $A^0 = Q$;
3. $(x, Q^1) \leftarrow next\_source(WQ)$;
4.   While x is not nil do
5.   — Let i = i+1;
6.   — Send Q^i to source x;
7.   — When x returns A^i, let $WQ = WQ\langle A^i \rangle$;
8.   — Let $(x, Q^{i+1}) \leftarrow next\_source(WQ)$;
9.   Return(A^i).
10. End

The procedure $source\_evaluate(Q)$ may return an incorrect answer when there are concurrent transactions at the sources that interfere with the query evaluation. For example, in Example 1, we saw that a delete that occurs at a source after a subquery has been evaluated there, but before the final answer is computed, may be skipped in the final query result. More subtle problems result when two subqueries of the same query are sent to the same source for evaluation at different times (to join with different relations) and use different source states, or when two subqueries are evaluated at two different sources in states that are inconsistent with each other. The key idea behind the Strobe algorithms is to keep track of the updates that occur during query evaluation, and to later compensate.

For simplicity, here we only consider insertions and deletions in our algorithms. Conceptually, modifications of tuples (updates sent to the warehouse) can be treated at the warehouse simply as a deletion of the old tuple followed by an insertion of the new tuple. However, for consistency and performance, the delete and the insert should be handled "at the same time." Our algorithms can be easily extended for this type of processing, but we do not do it here. Further discussion of how to treat a modification as an insert and a delete may be found in [11].

5.2.   Strobe

The Strobe algorithm processes updates as they arrive, sending queries to the sources when necessary. However, the updates are not performed immediately on the materialized view MV; instead, we generate a list of actions AL to be performed on the view. We update MV only when we are sure that applying all of the actions in AL (as a single transaction at the warehouse) will bring the view to a consistent state. This occurs when there are no outstanding queries and all received updates have been processed.

When the warehouse receives a deletion, it generates a delete action for the corresponding tuples (with matching key values) in MV. When an insert arrives, the warehouse may need to generate and process a query, using procedure $source\_evaluate()$. While a Q query is being answered by the sources, updates may arrive at the warehouse, and the answer obtained may have missed their effects. To compensate, we keep a set $pending(Q)$ of the updates that occur while Q is processed. After Q's answer is fully compensated, an insert action for MV is generated and placed on the action list AL.

Strobe algorithm

1. At each source:
2. ▷ After executing update U_i, send U_i to the warehouse.
3. ▷ Upon receipt of query Q_i, compute the answer A_i over $ss[x]$ (the current source state) and send A_i to the warehouse.
4. At the warehouse:
5. ▷ Initially, AL is set to empty $\langle\rangle$.
6. ▷ Upon receipt of update U_i:
7. o If U_i is a deletion
8. $\forall Q_j \in UQS$ add U_i to $pending(Q_j)$;
9. Add $key\_delete(MV, U_i)$ to AL.
10. o If U_i is an insertion
11. Let $Q_i = V\langle U_i\rangle$ and set $pending(Q_i) = \emptyset$;
12. Let $A_i = source\_evaluate(Q_i)$;
13. $\forall U_j \in pending(Q_i)$, apply $key\_delete(A_i, U_j)$;
14. Add insert(MV, A_i) to AL.
15. ▷ When $UQS = \emptyset$, apply AL to MV as a single transaction, without adding duplicate tuples to MV
16. Reset $AL = \langle\rangle$.
17. End Strobe algorithm.

Definition 4.   The unanswered query set UQS is the set of all queries that the warehouse has sent to some source but for which it has not yet received an answer.

Definition 5.   The operation $key\_delete(R, U_i)$ deletes from relation R the tuples whose key attributes have the same values as U_i.

Definition 6. $V\langle U\rangle$ denotes the view expression V with the tuple U substituted for U's relation.

The following example applies the Strobe algorithm to the warehouse scenario in Example 1 in the introduction. Specifically, it shows why a deletion needs to be applied to the answer of a previous query, when the previous query's answer arrives at the warehouse later than the deletion.

EXAMPLE 3:   Strobe avoids deletion anomaly
As in Example 1, let view V be defined as $V = r_1 \bowtie r_2 \bowtie r_3$, where r_1, r_2, r_3 are three relations residing on sources x, y and z, respectively. Initially, the relations are

$r_1:$	A	B		$r_2:$	B	C		$r_3:$	C	D
	1	2			-	-			3	4

The materialized view $MV = \emptyset$. We again consider two source updates: $U_1 = insert(r_2, [2, 3])$ and $U_2 = delete(r_1, [1, 2])$, and apply the Strobe algorithm.

1. $AL = \langle \rangle$. The warehouse receives $U_1 = insert(r_2, [2, 3])$ from source y. It generates query $Q_1 = r_1 \bowtie [2, 3] \bowtie r_3$. To evaluate Q_1, the warehouse first sends query $Q_1^1 = r_1 \bowtie [2, 3]$ to source x.

2. The warehouse receives $A_1^1 = [1, 2, 3]$ from source x. Query $Q_1^2 = [1, 2, 3] \bowtie r_3$ is sent to source z for evaluation.

3. The warehouse receives $U_2 = delete(r_1, [1, 2])$ from source x. It first adds U_2 to $pending(Q_1)$ and then adds $key\_delete(MV, U_2)$ to AL. The resulting $AL = \langle key\_delete(MV, U_2) \rangle$.

4. The warehouse receives $A_1^2 = [1, 2, 3, 4]$ from source z. Since $pending(Q)$ is not empty, the warehouse applies $key\_delete(A_1^2, U_2)$ and the resulting answer $A_2 = \emptyset$. Therefore, nothing is added to AL. There are no pending queries, so the warehouse updates MV by applying $AL = \langle key\_delete(MV, U_2) \rangle$. The resulting $MV = \emptyset$. The final view is correct and strongly consistent with the source relations.   □

This example demonstrates how Strobe avoids the anomaly that caused both ECA-key and conventional view maintenance algorithms to be incorrect: by remembering the delete until the end of the query, Strobe is able to correctly apply it to the query result *before* updating the view MV. If the deletion U_2 were received before Q_1^1 had been sent to source x, then A_1^1 would have been empty and no extra action would have been necessary.

The Strobe algorithm provides strong consistency for all single-update transaction environments. We prove the correctness of Strobe algorithm in Appendix A. Proof of Correctness for Strobe Algorithm.

6.   Transaction-Strobe and Global-Strobe

In this section we present two variations of the Strobe algorithm: T-Strobe that handles source-local transactions, and G-Strobe that handles global transactions.

6.1.   Transaction-Strobe algorithm

The Transaction-Strobe (T-Strobe) algorithm adapts the Strobe algorithm to provide strong consistency for source-local transactions. T-Strobe collects all of the updates performed by one transaction and processes these updates as a single unit. Batching the updates of a transaction not only makes it easier to enforce consistency, but also reduces the number of query messages that must be sent to and from the sources.

Definition 7. $UL(T)$ is the *update list* of a transaction T. $UL(T)$ contains the inserts and deletes performed by T, in order. $IL(T) \subseteq UL(T)$ is the *insertion list* of T; it contains all of the insertions performed by T.

Definition 8. $key(U_i)$ denotes the key attributes of the inserted or deleted tuple U_i.

The source actions in T-Strobe are the same as in Strobe; we therefore present only the warehouse actions. First, the warehouse removes all pairs of insertions and deletions such that the same tuple was first inserted and then deleted. This removal is an optimization that avoids sending out a query for the insertion, only to later delete the answer. Next the warehouse adds all remaining deletions to the action list AL. Finally, the warehouse generates one query for all of the insertions. As before, deletions which arrive at the warehouse after the query is generated are subtracted from the query result.

The following example demonstrates that the Strobe algorithm may only achieve convergence, while the T-Strobe algorithm guarantees strong consistency for source-local transactions. Because the Strobe algorithm does not understand transactions, it may provide a view which corresponds to the "middle" of a transaction at a source state. However, Strobe will eventually provide the correct view, once the transaction commits, and is therefore convergent.

EXAMPLE 4:   T-Strobe provides stronger consistency than Strobe

Consider a simple view over one source defined as $V = r_1$. Assume attribute A is the key of relation r_1. Originally, let the relation r_1 contain a single tuple $[1, 2]$. Initially $MV = ([1, 2])$. We consider one source transaction:

$$T_1 = \langle delete(r_1, [1, 2]), insert(r_1, [3, 4]) \rangle.$$

When the Strobe algorithm is applied to this scenario, the warehouse first adds the deletion to AL. Since there are no pending updates, AL is applied to MV and MV is updated to $MV = \emptyset$, which is not consistent with r_1 either before or after T_1. Then the warehouse processes the insertion and updates MV again, to the correct view $MV = ([3, 4])$.

Transaction-Strobe algorithm (T-Strobe)

1. At the warehouse:
2. $\triangleright$ Initially, $AL = \langle \rangle$.
3. $\triangleright$ Upon receipt of $UL(T_i)$ for a transaction T_i:
4. $\circ$ For each $U_j, U_k \in UL(T_i)$ such that U_j is an insertion, U_k is a deletion, $U_j < U_k$ and $key(U_j) = key(U_k)$, remove both U_j and U_k from $UL(T_i)$.
5. $\circ$ For every deletion $U \in UL(T_i)$:
6.   — $\forall Q_j \in UQS$, add U to $pending(Q_j)$.
7.   — Add $key\_delete(MV, U)$ to AL.
8. $\circ$ Let $Q_i = \bigcup_{U_j \in IL(T)} V\langle U_j \rangle$, and set $pending(Q_i) = \emptyset$;
9. $\circ$ Let $A_i = source\_evaluate(Q_i)$;
10. $\circ$ $\forall U \in pending(Q_i)$, apply $key\_delete(A_i, U)$;
11. $\circ$ Add $insert(MV, A_i)$ to AL.
12. $\triangleright$ When $UQS = \emptyset$, apply AL to MV, without adding duplicate tuples to MV. Reset $AL = \langle \rangle$.
13. End algorithm

The T-Strobe algorithm, on the other hand, only updates MV after both updates in the transaction have been processed. Therefore, MV is updated directly to the correct view, $MV = ([3, 4])$. □

The T-Strobe algorithm is inherently strongly consistent with respect to the source states defined after each source-local transaction[1]. T-Strobe can also process batched updates, not necessarily generated by the same transaction, but which were sent to the warehouse at the same time from the same source. In this case, T-Strobe also guarantees strong consistency if we define consistent source states to be those corresponding to the batching points at sources. Since it is common practice today to send updates from the sources periodically in batches, we believe that T-Strobe is probably the most useful algorithm. On single-update transactions, T-Strobe reduces to the Strobe algorithm.

6.2. Global-Strobe

While the T-Strobe algorithm is strongly consistent for source-local transactions, we show in the next example that it is only weakly consistent if global transactions are present. We then devise a new algorithm, Global-Strobe, to guarantee strong consistency for global transactions. Since the capabilities of the sources in a warehousing system may vary, we discuss several possible ways to create the Global-Strobe algorithm, based on the cooperativeness of the sources.

EXAMPLE 5:   T-Strobe with global transactions
Let the warehouse view V be defined as $V = r_1 \bowtie r_2$, where r_1, r_2 reside at sources x and y, respectively. Assume A is the key for r_1 and C is the key for r_2. Initially, the relations are:

r_1 :	A	B		r_2 :	B	C
	−	−			3	4
					3	5

The materialized view $MV = \emptyset$. $AL = \langle \rangle$. We consider two source transactions: $T_1 = \langle U_1 = insert(r_1, [1, 3]) \rangle$ and $T_2 = \langle U_2 = delete(r_2, [3, 4]), U_3 = insert(r_1, [2, 3]) \rangle$ and apply the T-Strobe algorithm.

1. The warehouse receives $U_1 = insert(r_1, [1, 3])$ from source x. It generates query $Q_1 = [1, 3] \bowtie r_2$ and sends Q_1 to source y for evaluation.

2. The warehouse receives $U_2 = delete(r_2, [3, 4])$ from source y[2]. Since U_2 belongs to a global transaction, it arrives at the warehouse with a transaction id attached. The warehouse temporarily stores U_2 in a holding queue, and does not process it until the remaining T_2 updates arrive.

3. The warehouse receives $A_1 = ([1, 3, 5])$ from source y. This answer was evaluated after U_2 occurred at source y. $Insert(MV, A_1)$ is added to AL. Because $UQS = \emptyset$, the warehouse applies AL to MV and $MV = ([1, 3, 5])$, which is a globally inconsistent state. (It is a weakly consistent state: the warehouse sees source x after T_1 but before T_2 and source y after both T_1 and T_2.)

4. The warehouse receives U_3 from source x, with an attached transaction id for T_2. Now that the T_2 updates have been fully received, T-Strobe adds $key\_delete(WC, U_2)$ to AL and sends query $Q_2 = [2, 3] \bowtie r_2$ to source y.

5. The warehouse receives $A_2 = ([2, 3, 5])$ from source y and adds $insert(MV, A_2)$ to AL. Since $UQS = \emptyset$, $AL = \langle key\_delete(MV, U_2), insert(MV, A_2) \rangle$ is applied to MV. The final MV is ([1,3,5], [2,3,5]), which is correct.   □

In step 3, above, the view is updated to a globally inconsistent state: $MV = ([1, 3, 5])$. The inconsistent state occurs because the evaluation of query Q_1 interferes with global transaction T_2. If the two actions in T_2 were treated as separate local transactions, then the state $MV = ([1, 3, 5])$ would be consistent with the source states after U_1 and U_2 (but before U_3). Therefore, T-Strobe is weakly but not strongly consistent in the presence of global transactions.

Example 5 shows that to achieve strong consistency, the warehouse needs to ensure that no global source transactions like T_2 are "pending" before it modifies the view. We now modify T-Strobe for the global transaction scenario, and create a new algorithm, Global-Strobe (G-strobe). Let TT be the set of transaction identifiers that the warehouse has received since it last updated MV. G-Strobe is the same as T-Strobe except that it only updates MV (with the actions in AL) when the following three conditions have all been met:

1. $UQS = \emptyset$;

2. For each transaction T_i in TT that depends on (in the concurrency control sense) another transaction T_j, T_j is also in TT; and

3. All of the updates of the transactions in TT have been received and processed.

When we apply the G-Strobe algorithm to the scenario in example 5, we see that now the warehouse will not update MV after processing T_1. Although at this point there are no unanswered queries, one update belonging to transaction T_2 has been received, which may have affected the evaluation of Q_1. Therefore, the warehouse delays updating MV until after receiving and processing all of T_2.

Enforcing condition 3, above, is easy if the sources cooperate, even when there is no global concurrency control. If all of the updates of a global transaction are sent in a single message by the committing site, then the warehouse will always have the entire transactions. If the updates are sent in separate messages, then transactions identifiers are needed in each message, plus a count of how many updates are involved in the transaction. Together, the count and identifiers make it possible for the warehouse to collect all of the updates before processing them.

Enforcing condition 2, above, may be more problematic in practice. Sources typically do not report the transactions on which a committing transaction depends. This means that condition 2 must be enforced indirectly. To illustrate, suppose transaction T_1 performs update U_{1x} at site x and U_{1y} at site y. Similarly, T_2 performs U_{2y} at y and U_{2z} at z. Assume that T_2 commits second and depends on T_1. If the updates are sent by the sources individually and in commit order, then the warehouse must receive U_{1y} before U_{2y}. Therefore, it is not possible to receive a transaction (e.g., T_2) without first receiving at least one of the updates of every transaction on which it depends (e.g., T_1), in the sense of transaction dependencies [4]. That is, condition 2 is automatically enforced.

If, on the other hand, site z reports all of the updates of T_2, then these updates could arrive before the warehouse receives any of T_1's updates. To enforce condition 2 in this scenario, we need to add sequence numbers to individual updates, and wait for all prior updates from a source. In our example, when T_2 is received, U_{2y} would contain a sequence number, say, 33. Then the warehouse would delay processing T_2 until all updates from source y with sequence numbers less than 33 (such as U_{1y}) arrive. This strategy is very conservative but does ensure condition 2.

In summary, the mechanism for sending transactions to the warehouse will determine if G-Strobe can reasonably guarantee strongly consistent views at the warehouse. If G-Strobe is not feasible, then we can revert to Strobe or T-Strobe and provide a weaker level of consistency. (Strobe only guarantees convergence for global transactions, as it does for source-local transactions. As we stated above, T-Strobe is weakly consistent for global transactions.)

7. Completeness and termination of the algorithms

A problem with Strobe, T-Strobe, and G-Strobe is that if there are continuous source updates, the algorithms may not reach a quiescent state where UQS is empty and the materialized view MV can be updated. To address this problem, in this section we present an algorithm, Complete Strobe (C-Strobe) that can update MV after any source update. For example, C-strobe can propagate updates to MV after a particular batch of updates has been received, or after some long period of time has gone by without a natural quiescent point. For simplicity, we will describe C-strobe enforcing an update to MV after each update; in this case, C-strobe achieves completeness. The extension to update MV after an arbitrary number of updates is straightforward and enforces strong consistency.

To force an update to MV after update U_i arrives at the warehouse, we need to compute the resulting view. However, other concurrent updates at the sources complicate the problem. In particular, consider the case where U_i is an insertion. To compute the next MV state, the warehouse sends a query Q_i to the sources. By the time the answer A_i arrives, the warehouse may have received (but not processed) updates $U_{i+1}...U_k$. Answer A_i may reflect the effects of these later updates, so before it can use A_i to update MV, the warehouse must "subtract out" the effects of later updates from A_i, or else it will not get a consistent state. If one of the later updates, say U_j, is an insert, then it can just remove the corresponding tuples from A_i. However, if U_j is a delete, the warehouse may need to *add* tuples to A_i, but to compute these missing tuples, it must send additional queries to the sources! When the answers to these additional queries arrive at the warehouse, they may also have to be adjusted for updates they saw but which should not be reflected in MV. Fortunately, as we show below, the process does converge, and eventually the warehouse is able to compute the consistent MV state that follows U_i. After it updates MV, the warehouse then processes U_{i+1} in the same fashion.

Before presenting the algorithm, we need a few definitions.

Definition 9. $Q_{i,-,-}$ denotes the set of queries sent by the warehouse to compute the view after insertion update U_i. $Q_{i,j,-}$ are the queries sent in response to update U_j that occurred while computing the answer for a query in $Q_{i,-,-}$. A unique integer k is used to distinguish each query in $Q_{i,j,-}$ as $Q_{i,j,k}$.

In the scenario above, for insert U_i we first generate $Q_{i,i,0}$. When its answer $A_{i,i,0}$ arrives, a deletion U_j received before $A_{i,i,0}$ requires us to send out another query, identified as Q_{i,j,new_j}. In the algorithm, new_j is used to generate the next unique integer for queries caused by U_j in the context of processing U_i.

When processing each update U_i separately, no action list AL is necessary. In the Strobe and T-strobe algorithms, AL keeps track of multiple updates whose processing overlaps. In the C-strobe algorithm outlined below, each update is compensated for subsequent, "held," updates so that it can be applied directly to the view. If C-strobe is extended (not shown here) to only force updates to MV periodically, after a batch of overlapping updates, then an action list AL is again necessary to remember the actions that should be applied for the entire batch.

Definition 10. $Q\langle U_i \rangle$ is the resulting query after the updated tuple in U_i replaces its base relation in Q. If the base relation of U_i does not appear in Q, then $Q\langle U_i \rangle = \emptyset$.

Definition 11. $Delta$ is the set of changes that need to be applied to MV for one insertion update. Note that $Delta$, when computed, would correspond to a single $insert(MV, Delta)$ action on AL if we kept an action list. (Deletion updates can be applied directly to MV, but insertions must be compensated first. $Delta$ collects the compensations.)

Definition 12.   Define $\Pi_{proj}(U_i)$ to be the tuple that agrees in all values with tuple of update U_i, but only has those attributes of U_i that appears in the list *proj*.

We also use a slightly different version of *key_delete*: $key\_delete^*(Delta, U_k)$ only deletes from $Delta$ those tuples that match with U_k on both key and non-key attributes (not just on key attributes). Finally, when we add tuples to $Delta$, we assume that tuples with the same key values but different non-key values will be added. These tuples violate the key condition, but only appear in $Delta$ temporarily. However, it is important to keep them in $Delta$ for the algorithm to work correctly. (The reason for these changes is that when we "subtract out" the updates seen by $Q_{i,i,0}$, we first compensate for deletes, and then for all inserts. In between, we may have two tuples with the same key, one added from the compensation of a delete, and the other to be deleted when we compensate for inserts.) We present the warehouse C-Strobe algorithm, the source behavior remains the same as for the Strobe algorithm.

C-Strobe is complete because MV is updated once after each update, and the resulting warehouse state corresponds to the source state after the same update. We prove the correctness of C-Strobe in Appendix B. Proof of Correctness for Complete Strobe Algorithm.

The compensating process (the loop in the algorithm) always terminates because any expression $Q_{i,j,k}\langle U_p \rangle$ always has one fewer base relation than $Q_{i,j,k}$. Let us assume that there are at most K updates that can arrive between the time a query is sent out and its answer is received, and that there are n base relations. When we process insertion U_i we send out query $Q_{i,i,0}$; when we get its answer we may have to send out at most K compensating queries with $n-2$ base relations each. For each of those queries, at most K queries with $n-3$ base relations may be sent, and so on. Thus, the total number of queries sent in the loop is no more than K^{n-2}, and the algorithm eventually finishes processing U_i and updates MV.

The number of compensating queries may be significantly reduced by combining related queries. For example, when we compensate for $Q_{i,i,0}$, the above algorithm sends out up to K queries. However, since there are only n base relations, we can group these queries into $n-1$ queries, where each combined query groups all of the queries generated by an update to the same base relation. If we continue to group queries by base relation, we see that the total number of compensating queries cannot exceed $(n-1) \times (n-2) \times \ldots \times 1 = (n-1)!$. That is, C-Strobe will update MV after at most $(n-1)!$ queries are evaluated. If the view involves a small number of relations, then this bound will be relatively small. Of course, this maximum number of queries only occurs under extreme conditions where there is a continuous stream of updates.

Complete Strobe algorithm(C-Strobe)

1. At the warehouse:
2.   ▷ Initially, $Delta = \emptyset$.
3.   ▷ As updates arrive, they are placed in a holding queue.
4.   ▷ We process each update U_i in order of arrival:
5.   ○ If U_i is a deletion
6.   Apply $key\_delete(MV, U_i)$.
7.   ○ If U_i is an insertion
8.   — Let $Q_{i,i,0} = V\langle U_i \rangle$;
9.   — Let $A_{i,i,0} = source\_evaluate(Q_{i,i,0})$;
10.   — Repeat for each $A_{i,j,k}$ until $UQS = \emptyset$:
11.   Add $A_{i,j,k}$ to $Delta$ (without adding duplicate tuples).
12.   For all deletions U_p received between U_j and $A_{i,j,k}$:
13.   Let $Q_{i,p,new_p} = Q_{i,j,k}\langle U_p \rangle$;
14.   Let $A_{i,p,new_p} = source\_evaluate(Q_{i,p,new_p})$;
15.   When answer arrives, processing starts from line 10.
16.   — For all insertions U_k received between U_i and the last answer, if $\neg\exists U_j < U_k$ such that U_j is a deletion and $\Pi_{proj}(U_j) = \Pi_{proj}(U_k)$, then apply $key\_delete^*(Delta, U_k)$.
17.   — Let $MV = MV + Delta$ and $Delta = \emptyset$.
18. End algorithm.

We now apply the C-Strobe algorithm to the warehouse scenario in Example 1, and show how C-Strobe processes this scenario differently from the Strobe algorithm (shown in Example 3).

EXAMPLE 6: C-Strobe applied to example of introduction

As in examples 1 and 3, let view V be defined as $V = r_1 \bowtie r_2 \bowtie r_3$, where r_1, r_2, r_3 are three relations residing on sources x, y and z, respectively. Initially, the relations are

$$r_1 : \frac{A \quad B}{1 \quad 2} \qquad r_2 : \frac{B \quad C}{- \quad -} \qquad r_3 : \frac{C \quad D}{3 \quad 4}$$

The materialized view $MV = \emptyset$. We again consider two source updates: $U_1 = insert(r_2, [2, 3])$ and $U_2 = delete(r_1, [1, 2])$, and apply the C-Strobe algorithm. There are two possible orderings of events at the warehouse. Here we consider one, and in the next example we discuss the other.

1. $Delta = \emptyset$. The warehouse receives $U_1 = insert(r_2, [2, 3])$ from source y. It generates query $Q_{1,1,0} = r_1 \bowtie [2, 3] \bowtie r_3$. To evaluate $Q_{1,1,0}$, the warehouse first sends query $Q_{1,1,0}^1 = r_1 \bowtie [2, 3]$ to source x.

2. The warehouse receives $A_{1,1,0}^1 = [1, 2, 3]$ from source x. Query $Q_{1,1,0}^2 = [1, 2, 3] \bowtie r_3$ is sent to source z for evaluation.

3. The warehouse receives $U_2 = delete(r_1, [1, 2])$ from source x. It saves this update in a queue.

4. The warehouse receives $A_{1,1,0} = A_{1,1,0}^2 = ([1, 2, 3, 4])$ from source z, which is the final answer to $Q_{1,1,0}$. Since U_2 was received between $Q_{1,1,0}$ and $A_{1,1,0}$ and it is a deletion, the warehouse generates a query $Q_{1,2,1} = [1, 2] \bowtie [2, 3] \bowtie r_3$ and sends it to source z. Also, it adds $A_{1,1,0}$ to $Delta$, so $Delta = ([1, 2, 3, 4])$.

5. The warehouse receives $A_{1,2,1} = ([1, 2, 3, 4])$ and tries to add it to $Delta$. Since it is a duplicate tuple, $Delta$ remains the same.

6. $UQS = \emptyset$, so the warehouse updates the view to $MV = MV + Delta = ([1, 2, 3, 4])$.

7. Next the warehouse processes U_2 which is next in the update queue. Since U_2 is a deletion, it applies $key\_delete^*(MV, U_2)$ and $MV = \emptyset$. □

In this example, MV is updated twice, in steps 6 and 7. After step 6, MV is equal to the result of evaluating V after U_1 but before U_2 occurs. Similarly, after step 7, MV corresponds to evaluating V after U_2, but before any further updates occur, which is the final source state in this example. In the next example we consider the case where U_2 occurs before the evaluation of the query corresponding to U_1, and we show that compensating queries are necessary.

EXAMPLE 7: C-Strobe applied again, with different timing of the updates

Let the view definition, initial base relations and source updates be the same as in example 6. We now consider a different set of events at the warehouse.

1. $Delta = \emptyset$. The warehouse receives $U_1 = insert(r_2, [2, 3])$ from source y. It generates query $Q_{1,1,0} = r_1 \bowtie [2, 3] \bowtie r_3$. To evaluate $Q_{1,1,0}$, the warehouse first sends query $Q^1_{1,1,0} = r_1 \bowtie [2, 3]$ to source x.

2. The warehouse receives $U_2 = delete(r_1, [1, 2])$ from source x. It saves this update in a queue.

3. The warehouse receives $A^1_{1,1,0} = \emptyset$ from source x. This implies that $A_{1,1,0} = \emptyset$. Since U_2 was received between $Q_{1,1,0}$ and $A_{1,1,0}$, the warehouse generates the compensating query $Q_{1,2,1} = [1, 2] \bowtie [2, 3] \bowtie r_3$ and sends it to source z. Also, it adds $A_{1,1,0}$ to $Delta$ and $Delta$ is still empty.

4. The warehouse receives $A_{1,2,1} = ([1, 2, 3, 4])$ and adds it to $Delta$. $Delta = ([1, 2, 3, 4])$.

5. Since $UQS = \emptyset$, the warehouse updates the view to $MV = MV + Delta = ([1, 2, 3, 4])$.

6. The warehouse processes U_2. Since U_2 is a deletion, it applies $key\_delete^*(MV, U_2)$ and $MV = \emptyset$.   □

The algorithm C-Strobe is complete. We give the proof of correctness in Appendix B. Proof of Correctness for Complete Strobe Algorithm.

As mentioned earlier, C-Strobe can be extended to update MV periodically, after processing $k > 1$ updates. In this case, we periodically stop processing updates (placing them in a holding queue). We then process the answers to all queries that are in UQS as we did in C-Strobe, and then apply the action list AL to the view MV. The T-Strobe algorithm can also be made complete or periodic in a similar way. We call this algorithm C-TStrobe, but do not describe it here further.

8. Implementation of the Strobe family of algorithms

The Strobe family of algorithms, including Strobe, T-Strobe and C-Strobe are implemented in the WHIPS prototype (WareHousing Information Project at Stanford)[26]. Figure 2 shows the architecture of the WHIPS system. Each box in the figure is a module that performs a specific function. Each module is implemented as a CORBA object. They communicate with each other using ILU, a COBRA compliant object library developed by Xerox PARC[8]. Different modules can reside on different machines and can be implemented in different language. Similar to a real-world data warehousing system, data sources are separated from the integration modules, and the warehouse is a separate database which may or may not be closely coupled with the integration components.

In WHIPS, views are defined through a *view specifier* using an SQL-like view definition language. When defining a view, the desired consistency level of this view is specified. For example, a clause "**with** strong **consistency**" specifies that the current view will be maintained in a strongly consistent fashion. When the *integrator* receives a view definition, it spawns a *view manager* that executes the required consistency algorithm. For example, the Strobe algorithm is implemented in a Strobe view manager that maintains a view requiring strong consistency. When the system is running, one view manager maintains one view.

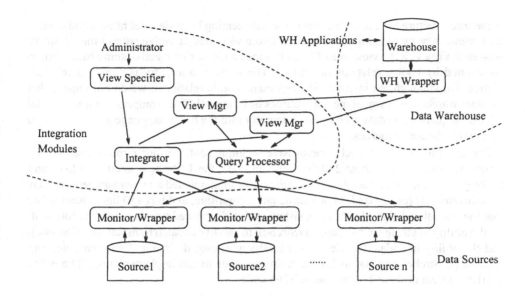

Figure 2. The WHIPS system architecture

After a view is initialized and stored at the warehouse, *source monitors* detect changes on the source data and notify the integrator [19]. The integrator then forwards source updates to the relevant view managers.

All view managers work concurrently to maintain their own view. A view manager manages source updates and maintains data structures for view maintenance. For example, a Strobe view manager maintains UQS and $pending(Q)$ (the pending delete queue) required by the algorithm. A view manager sends proper queries to the *query processor* and receives answers to those queries. Then it may perform some post processing on the answers and decide when to update the materialized view. It sends an *action list* to the warehouse wrapper to initialize or modify a materialized view.

The query processor basically implements the procedure $source\_evaluate()$ required by the Strobe algorithms. It receives global queries from the view managers and poses the appropriate single-source queries to the source wrappers to answer them. It then passes the composite global query answers back to the view managers. In our current implementation, the query processor uses standard techniques such as sideways information passing and filtering of selection conditions to prune the queries it poses to the wrappers. Because of the modularity of the WHIPS system, other query processing techniques can be added to the query processor without affecting other parts of the system. There could also be more than one query processor if necessary. The *warehouse wrapper* receives action lists from the view managers and executes the desired actions on views. All modifications received by the warehouse wrapper in a single message are applied to the warehouse in one transaction, as needed by the view consistency algorithms.

The implementation of the Strobe family algorithms is straightforward given the pseudo-code we have presented. We use *view tree*, an internal representation which is basically a parse tree structure for a relational view, for representing both view definitions and queries on a view. A view definition is translated into a view tree at initialization time. A query related to view V is the view tree of V with some conditions changed or some base relation substituted by known relations or tuples. The answer to a query is simply a relation. Notice that although our internal view representation is relational, we do not require that the data warehouse or any of the data sources be relational. The wrappers can translate the relational queries and data used by the integrator into the native language and model used by the warehouse or sources.

The algorithms are relatively inexpensive to implement. In our implementation, the Strobe view manager is about 250 lines of C++ code, the T-Strobe is about 350 lines and C-Strobe is about 400 lines. As a comparison, we implemented a view manager that runs the conventional (centralized) view maintenance algorithm, and it is 150 lines. Remember that the centralized algorithm is inconsistent in this distributed warehousing environment. So the ability to guarantee correctness (Strobe), the ability to batch transactions (T-Strobe), and the ability to update the view consistently, whenever desired and without quiescing updates (C-Strobe) cost 100 to 250 extra lines of code in this implementation. The entire WHIPS system is about 12,000 lines of C++ code.

9. Conclusions

In this paper, we identified three fundamental transaction processing scenarios for data warehousing and developed the Strobe family of algorithms to consistently maintain the warehouse data. Figure 3 summarizes the algorithms we discussed in this paper and their correctness. In the figure, "Conventional" refers to a conventional centralized view maintenance algorithm, while "ECA" and "ECA-Key" are algorithms from [28].

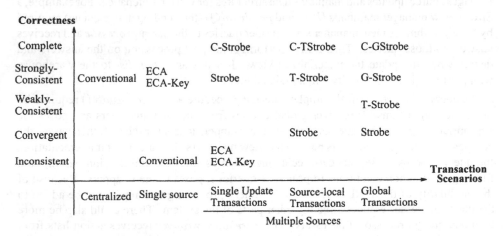

Figure 3. Consistency Spectrum

In Figure 3, an algorithm is shown in a particular scenario S and level of consistency L if it achieves L consistency in scenario S. Furthermore, the algorithm at (S, L) also achieves all lower levels of consistency for S, and achieves L consistency for scenarios that are less restrictive than S (scenarios to the left of S). For example, Strobe is strongly consistent for single update transactions at multiple sources. Therefore, it is weakly consistent and convergent (by definition) in that scenario. Similarly, Strobe is strongly consistent for centralized and single source scenarios.

Regarding the efficiency of the algorithms we have presented, there are three important points to make. First, there are a variety of enhancements that can improve efficiency substantially:

1. We can optimize global query evaluation. For example, in the procedure $source\_evaluate()$, the warehouse can group all queries for one source into one, or can find an order of sources that minimizes data transfers.

2. We can find the optimal batch size for processing. By batching together updates, we can reduce the message traffic to and from sources. However, delaying update processing means the warehouse view will not be as up to date, so there is a clear tradeoff that we would like to explore.

3. We can use key information to avoid sending some queries to sources [15]. For example, suppose the view definition is $V = r_1 \bowtie r_2$, r_1 has attributes A, B, and r_2 has attributes B, C. Further suppose that the current MV contains tuple $[1, 2, 3]$ and we know that B is a key for r_2. If the warehouse receives an update $U_1 = insert(r_1, [4, 2])$, there is no need to send the query $[4, 2] \bowtie r_2$ to the source containing r_2. Because B is the key for r_2, and because the view contains $[1, 2, 3]$, we know that r_2 must contain $[2, 3]$. Therefore, we need to add (exactly) the tuple $[4, 2, 3]$ to the view.

4. Although we argued against keeping copies of *all* base relations at the warehouse, it may make sense to copy the most frequently accessed ones (or portions thereof), if they are not too large or expensive to keep up to date. This also increases the number of queries that can be answered locally.

The second point regarding efficiency is that, even if someone determines that none of these algorithms is efficient enough for their application, it is still very important to understand the tradeoffs involved. The Strobe algorithms exemplify the inherent cost of keeping a warehouse consistent. Given these costs, users can now determine what is best for them, given their consistency requirements and their transactional scenario.

Third, when updates arrive infrequently at the warehouse, or only in periodic batches with large gaps in between, the Strobe algorithms are as efficient as conventional algorithms such as those in [5]. They only introduce extra complexity when updates must be processed while other updates are arriving at the warehouse, which is when conventional algorithms cannot guarantee a consistent view.

Recall that in Section 3 we made a critical "event ordering" assumption. This assumption states that sources report events in the correct order. As we stated, if legacy sources cannot guarantee this, then it is impossible to guarantee any type of correctness. However, if the sources only report updates in the correct order (but may report query answers in any order with respect to the updates), then we can still achieve eventual consistency (i.e., guarantee convergence). There are two cases to consider: (1) an answer A_i arrives at the warehouse *before* an update U_j that is already reflected in A_i, and (2) A_i is computed before U_j occurs at a source, but A_i arrives at the warehouse *after* U_j does. The first case may cause the warehouse to compute an incorrect materialized view, but eventually, when U_j arrives, the view will be corrected. Therefore, the warehouse can still guarantee convergence. The Strobe algorithms already handles the second case by using $pending(Q_i)$, and also guarantee convergence at the end of processing both Q_i and U_j. If we make the reasonable assumption that concurrent answers and updates will arrive soon after each other, if not in the correct order, then the warehouse will not diverge far from a consistent state, will always return to a consistent state, and will do so fairly quickly.

As part of our ongoing warehousing work, we are currently evaluating the performance of the Strobe and T-Strobe algorithms, and considering some of the optimizations mentioned above. We are also extending the algorithms to handle more general type of views, for example, views with insufficient key information, and views defined by more complex relational algebra expressions.

Our future work includes designing maintenance algorithms that coordinate updates to multiple warehouse views [29].

Acknowledgments

We would like to thank Jennifer Widom and Jose Blakely for discussions that led to some of the ideas in this paper.

Appendix A. Proof of Correctness for Strobe Algorithm

The Strobe algorithm provides strong consistency for all single-update transaction environments. In this section we outline a proof for the Strobe algorithm. The intuition is that each time MV is modified, updates have quiesced and the view contents can be obtained by evaluating the view expression at the current source states. Therefore, although not all source states will be reflected in the view, the view always reflects a consistent set of source states. We note that the ECA-key algorithm in [28] does not always process deletions correctly even in a single source environment. The problem occurs when the deleted tuple is the same as an inserted tuple participating in an ongoing query. The Strobe algorithm corrects this error and processes all updates correctly.

THEOREM 1 *The Strobe algorithm is strongly consistent.*

Proof: Assume that the warehouse receives and processes updates in the order $U_1, U_2, \ldots$. In this scenario, each update represents a source transaction, so let R be the serial schedule where transactions are executed in this order. Notice that R must be equivalent to the actual schedule executed at the sources, S. If transactions at a particular source x are executed in a given order, this must be the order in R because the Strobe algorithm processes updates in the order received. Transactions from different sources may appear in a different order in R, but this does not matter since they do not conflict (the transaction access data at different sites).

To illustrate, assume two updates U_{1x}, U_{2x} occur at source x in that order and update U_{1y} occurs at source y. Assume the source schedule is $S = U_{1x}, U_{2x}, U_{1y}$, but updates arrive at the warehouse in the order $R = U_{1x}, U_{1y}, U_{2x}$. Since U_{1y} and U_{2x} do not conflict they can be swapped, and the two schedules are equivalent.

Now that we have defined the schedule R required by the strong consistency definition, let us define the mapping m. Consider a warehouse state ws_x where $UQS = \emptyset$. Say that at this point the Strobe algorithm has processed updates U_1 through U_k inclusive. We map ws_x into ss_k, where $ss_k = result(U_1, \ldots, U_k)$.

Now we must show that $V[ss_k] = V[ws_x]$. We do this by contradiction, i.e., assume that $V[ss_k] \neq V[ws_x]$. Then there must be a tuple t that is either missing from $V[ws_x]$ or is an extra tuple in $V[ws_x]$. (In what follows, we do not have to worry about t appearing more than once either at the source or the warehouse due to our key condition.) We also know that $V[ss_0] = V[ws_0]$, where ss_0 is the initial source state and ws_0 is the initial warehouse state. There are two main cases to consider.

Case I: $t \in V[ss_k]$ and $t \notin V[ws_x]$.

Subcase I(a): There is (at least one) insert at the source that generates t. Let U_i be the last of these inserts that are processed at the warehouse. Insert U_i adds a tuple that contains one of the keys involved in t to some relation at a source. (Recall that t has a key value for each of the relations involved in the view definition.) There can be no deletes involving a t key after U_i and before U_k. If there were, they would remove t from $V[ss_k]$, a contradiction.

Under Strobe, U_i gets propagated to the warehouse, a query Q is generated, evaluated using source relations, and an answer returned to the warehouse. At the warehouse, both the processing of U_i and the receipt of the Q answer must occur before or at state ws_x. (U_i cannot be received after ws_x since we are assuming that U_i is a processed update. If the Q answer arrived after ws_x, then UQS would not have been empty at this state.) When Q is processed at the source, it sees all the key values involved in t, so the answer to Q contains t. Thus, t is inserted into the materialized view. Because there are no subsequent deletes affecting t at the source between the processing of U_i and U_k, t remains until ws_x, a contradiction.

Subcase I(b): There are no inserts at the source that generate t. This means that t must have been in $V[ss_0]$, and thus in $V[ws_0]$. Similarly to Case I(a), there are no deletes affecting t at the source before ss_k (otherwise t could not be in $V[ss_k]$) and hence no such deletes at the warehouse. Thus, t remains at the warehouse, a contradiction.

Case II: $t \notin V[ss_k]$ and $t \in V[ws_x]$.

Subcase II(a): There is at least one delete at some source that involves a t key value. The proof is analogous to Case I(a). We consider the last such source delete U_d processed at the warehouse. Clearly, the warehouse deletes t from the materialized view when processing U_d. Since $t \in V[ws_x]$, it must have been reinserted. Notice that there are no inserts that could generate t at the source after U_d, so there cannot be any corresponding inserts that warehouse. However, it could be the case that an insert U_j occurring at the source *before* U_d, could generate an answer that is processed at the warehouse *after* U_d. In Strobe, all such queries are processed by *key-delete*(Q_j, U_d). This deletes tuple t from the answer if it was there. Thus, there is no way the answer could contain t when it is added to MV, this is a contradiction.

Subcase II(b): There are no source deletes that involve a key value of t. Therefore t must not be in the initial $V[ss_0]$, and since the initial materialized view is correct, t is not in $V[ws_0]$. Since somehow t appears in $V[ws_x]$, it must have been inserted by some answer received at the warehouse. Say ss_l is the source state right after the answer is generated. At that point $V[ss_l]$ must contain t. Since there are no deletes affecting t at the source, then t remains, a contradiction.

We have now shown that $V[ss_k] = V[ws_x]$. Since the materialized view only changes at the warehouse when $UQS = \emptyset$, this completes the first part of the proof that Strobe is strongly consistent. For the second part we must show that if we have two warehouse states, ws_g and ws_x, where $g < f$, then the source states they map to occur in this same order. Let U_j be the last update processed at the warehouse at ws_g and U_k be the last update at ws_x. Clearly, $j < k$, so source state ss_j will occur before state ss_k as R is executed. This completes the proof. ■

Appendix B. Proof of Correctness for Complete Strobe Algorithm

We prove the completeness of C-Strobe by enumerating update scenarios and studying possible view contents.

THEOREM 2 *The Complete Strobe (C-Strobe) algorithm is complete.*

Proof: C-Strobe processes updates in the order of their arrival. Assume that the list of updates at the warehouse in their processing order is $U_1, U_2, \ldots$. Let R be the serial schedule where transactions are executed in this order. As we argued in Section A. Proof of Correctness for Strobe Algorithm, R is a serial source schedule that is equivalent to the actual execution, and R will serve as the serial schedule required by the proof of complete consistency. Let the warehouse state after processing U_x be ws_x and let the source state $ss_x = result(U_1, \ldots, U_x)$, ss_x is a consistent source state.

Let $MV[ws_x]$ be the materialized view at state ws_x. $MV[ws_x]$ is the same as $V[ws_x]$ in the consistency definition, we use $MV[ws_x]$ here because MV is used in the algorithm. We know that $MV[ws_0] = V[ss_0]$. Again, C-Strobe receives updates from sources, stores them in the order of their arrival and processes one update at a time (line 4 to line 17). We call the update U_i in line 4 the *current update*, and all the discussions below are within the context of processing U_i. Assume we have $MV[ws_{i-1}] = V[ss_{i-1}]$. That is, MV at state ws_{i-1} correctly reflects the source state ss_{i-1}. We prove by induction that $MV[ws_i] = V[ss_i]$, $MV[ws_i]$ is the materialized view after processing U_i using C-Strobe.

Case I: If U_i is a deletion, then the deletion is applied to MV directly. By inductive hypothesis we know that before applying U_i, MV is the same as $V[ss_{i-1}]$. After applying the deletion, $MV[ws_i]$ is $MV[ws_{i-1}]$ with all tuples whose keys agree with U_i deleted. At the same time, $V[ss_i]$ is $V[ss_{i-1}]$ with all tuples whose keys agree with U_i deleted. By the key assumption, one tuple in the view has only one derivation from the base relations. So $MV[ws_i] = V[ss_i]$.

Case II: When U_i is an insertion, we know from basic incremental view update theory that $V[ss_i] = V[ss_{i-1}] \cup V\langle U_i\rangle[ss_{i-1}]$. That is, the correct view increment corresponding to U_i is $V\langle U_i\rangle$ evaluated at source state ss_{i-1}. From the algorithm we have $MV[ws_i] = MV[ws_{i-1}] \cup Delta$. That is, the answer to $Q_{i,i,0}$ and the results of all following compensating queries and actions are stored in $Delta$ when MV is updated. The expression we want to prove is:

$$V[ss_{i-1}] \cup V\langle U_i\rangle[ss_{i-1}] = MV[ws_{i-1}] \cup Delta \qquad (B.1)$$

Following we first prove that $V\langle U_i\rangle[ss_{i-1}] \subset Delta$, then we prove that $Delta \subset MV[ws_{i-1}] \cup V\langle U_i\rangle[ss_{i-1}]$. The two cases will lead us to prove expression (B.1).

Case II(a): All tuples in $V\langle U_i\rangle[ss_{i-1}]$ are in $Delta$.

A query Q sent by C-Strobe could be either the initial query corresponding to U_i (line 8), or one of compensating queries that is caused by a deletion U_d (line 13). In either case, one query Q is directly triggered by one update U. (U is U_i in the first case and U_d in the second case.) Q is intended to be evaluated at the moment when it is sent out, i.e., at the source state with no further updates occurring after U. If there are actually updates after U, then first (line 12-15) deletions among those updates are compensated by sending compensating queries, second (line 16) insertions are compensated by deleting those extra tuples introduced.

Assume t is a tuple in $V\langle U_i\rangle[ss_{i-1}]$. First, we prove that t should be in $Delta$ after all deletions are compensated (when the algorithm reaches line 16). Let $BT(t)$ be the set of *base relation tuples* that derive view tuple t. For example, say we have base relations $R(A, B)$, $S(B, C)$, with A and B as keys of R and S, respectively. If R contains a single tuple $[1, 2]$ and S contains a single tuple $[2, 3]$, and we have $V = \Pi_{A,B}(R \bowtie S)$, then $[1, 2]$ is a view tuple and $BT([1, 2]) = \{[1, 2], [2, 3]\}$. As we can see, different sets of base tuples may derive the same view tuple. However, because of our key constraints on view definitions, a view tuple has only one derivation at a given time. We consider the following three scenarios:

1. There are no further updates after the warehouse receives U_i and before it receives $A_{i,i,0}$. As a result of the event order assumption 3.3, no update *occurred* after U_i and before the evaluation of the answer. Since $A_{i,i,0}$ is the intended results for $Q_{i,i,0} = V\langle U_i\rangle$,

   That means $Q_{i,i,0}$ was evaluated in state ss_{i-1}. So $A_{i,i,0} = V\langle U_i\rangle[ss_{i-1}]$ and t is in $A_{i,i,0}$. Since $A_{i,i,0}$ is added to $Delta$ in line 11, t should be in $Delta$ when the algorithm reaches line 16.

2. There are no deletions of those tuple in $BT(t)$ between the receipt of U_i and the receipt of $A_{i,i,0}$. In this scenario, t should be in $A_{i,i,0}$. Insertions and deletions of tuples not in $BT(t)$ do not affect the existence of t in $A_{i,i,0}$. As argued above, t is added to $Delta$.

3. At least one tuple in $BT(t)$ is deleted from a base relation after U_i and before the receipt of $A_{i,i,0}$. In this scenario, tuple t may be missing from $A_{i,i,0}$. Let $Q_{i,i,0}$ be query X_1. According to C-Strobe, a query $Q_{i,k,x}$ is sent corresponding to U_k. Let query $Q_{i,k,x}$ be X_2. In query X_2, U_k is provided (as well as U_i). If there are no more deletions of tuple in $BT(t)$ after X_2 is sent, then because U_i and U_k are present in the query and other tuples in $BT(t)$ are

still in the base relations, tuple t will be contained in the answer of X_2. Therefore, t is added to $Delta$.

When the answer of query X_2 is received, either we have t in the answer and add it to $Delta$, or another query X_3 which contains U_i, U_k and another tuple in $BT(t)$ will be generated. We could make similar arguments in the situation where there are further deletions of tuples in $BT(t)$ before finish the entire processing of U_i. This process repeats until either

(A) There are no deletions of tuples in $BT(t)$ between sending a query X_l and receiving its answer. In this case, tuple t is contained in the answer of X_l and added to $Delta$.

(B) Query X_l contains all tuples in $BT(t)$. We know this will happen because each time C-Strobe generates a compensating query (line 13) it adds one known tuple into the original query. So X_{l+1} always contains one more tuple than X_l and that tuple is in $BT(t)$. We know that X_1 contains $n - 1$ base relations (n is the number of base relations in the view definition). So query X_l will contain $n - l$ base relations, and $X_n (l = n)$ has only known tuples from $BT(t)$. Thus, X_n can be evaluated locally at the warehouse. Further deletions of tuples in $BT(t)$ from base relations do affect the answer of X_n. Since all tuples in $BT(t)$ are carried by X_n, tuple t is guaranteed to be in the answer of X_n, and thus, in $Delta$.

Notice that to keep all potential tuples in $Delta$, we need to let $Delta$ take tuples with the same key values but different non-key values. To see this, suppose that at a given time a tuple t is missing from $Delta$ because a deletion U_d caused the answer that was to contain t to be incomplete. A compensation query Q_d was sent as a result of U_d. However, before the answer of Q_d arrives, an insertion into a base relation may derive a tuple t' which has the same key value with t. Tuple t' may be brought to the warehouse by another answer relation and be added into $Delta$ before t. If t' does not agree with t on non-key values, then it may be removed from $Delta$ when compensating inserts later. However, t should remain in $Delta$. Therefore, at this point we should keep both t and t' in $Delta$ and should not reject t because there is a tuple in $Delta$ with the same key value.

Now we have shown that after processing all the deletions, all tuples in the view increment $V\langle U_i\rangle[ss_{i-1}]$ are in $Delta$. Next, we argue that no "useful" tuple t can be deleted accidently when processing further insertions (in line 16). Consider an insertion U_k into relation R that is received before we finish processing U_i. U_k is compensated for in line 16. Let t be a tuple in $V\langle U_i\rangle[ss_{i-1}]$,

1. If $U_k \notin BT(t)$, then $key\_delete^*(Delta, U_k)$ will not delete tuple t from $Delta$.

2. If $U_k \in BT(t)$ and U_k is an insert into relation R_1. Since t was in $V\langle U_i\rangle[ss_{i-1}]$, in state ss_{i-1} there must be an R_1 tuple t_1 that matches U_k in all the attributes in the *proj* list, that is, $\Pi_{proj}(t_1) = \Pi_{proj}(U_k)$. Tuple t_1 is not in R_1 when U_k occurs at the source (otherwise the insertion U_k will fail since U_k and t have the same projected attributes, including key attributes.) Therefore, t_1 must have been deleted before U_k. In this case, $key\_delete^*(Delta, U_k)$ is not applied and t remains in $Delta$.

Case II(b): All tuples in $Delta$ must be either in $V\langle U_i \rangle[ss_{i-1}]$, or in $MV[ws_{i-1}]$.

Tuples in $Delta$ all came from answers of the queries (line 11). We consider the following three scenarios:

1. When there are no updates after U_i and before we finish processing U_i. In this scenario, $Delta = A_{i,i,0} = V\langle U_i \rangle[ss_{i-1}]$.

2. There are only deletions after U_i.

   We know from the above discussions that a query Q is always directly triggered by an update U (U_i or U_d). Let the *intended answer* of Q be the answer relation if Q is evaluated at the source state when there is no update after U. Let the *actual answer* of Q be the answer relation the warehouse receives when it executes C-Strobe. When there are only deletions after U_i, it is clear that the actual answer of any query can only have *less* tuples than the intended answer. In the following we show that any *intended answer* of queries sent by C-Strobe is a subset of $V\langle U_i \rangle[ss_{i-1}]$. Then the sum of all actual answers, which is a subset of all intended answers, is also a subset of $V\langle U_i \rangle[ss_{i-1}]$. $Delta$ is the sum of all the actual answers.

   From item 1 above we know that for $Q_{i,i,0}$, the intended answer is the same as $V\langle U_i \rangle[ss_{i-1}]$.

   Any compensating query (sent at line 13) is obtained from substituting one base relation by a deleted tuple from a previous query. So a compensating query must have the following format:
   $$Q = V\langle U_i, U_{d_1}, U_{d_2} \ldots U_{d_k} \rangle$$
   $$= \Pi_{proj}(\sigma_{cond}(U_i \bowtie U_{d_1} \bowtie U_{d_2} \ldots U_{d_k} \bowtie r_{b_1} \bowtie r_{b_2} \bowtie \ldots \bowtie r_{b_n}))$$
   In this query expression, U_i is the current update, U_{d_j}s are deletions received after U_i, and r_{b_j}s are base relations. Notice that all the known tuples in the join expression have been placed before all base relations just for convenience. Assume U_{d_k} is the update that triggers query Q (and it is the last of all those deletions). The intended answer of Q is the answer of the expression evaluated right after U_{d_k} occurs.
   $$A_{int} = \Pi_{proj}(\sigma_{cond}(U_i \bowtie U_{d_1} \bowtie U_{d_2} \ldots U_{d_k} \bowtie r_{b_1}[ss_{d_k}]$$
   $$\bowtie r_{b_2}[ss_{d_k}] \bowtie \ldots \bowtie r_{b_n}[ss_{d_k}]))$$
   At the same time, we have
   $$V\langle U_i \rangle[ss_{i-1}] = \Pi_{proj}(\sigma_{cond}(U_i \bowtie r_{d_1}[ss_{i-1}] \bowtie r_{d_2}[ss_{i-1}] \ldots r_{d_k}[ss_{i-1}]$$
   $$\bowtie r_{b_1}[ss_{i-1}] \bowtie r_{b_2}[ss_{i-1}] \bowtie \ldots \bowtie r_{b_n}[ss_{i-1}]))$$
   In this expression, r_{d_j} is the corresponding base relation of U_{d_j}. Since we know $U_{d_j} \in r_{d_j}$ (only delete existing tuple) and $r_{b_j}[ss_{d_k}] \subset r_{b_j}[ss_{i-1}]$ (tuples are deleted from the relation), we can infer that $A_{int} \in V\langle U_i \rangle[ss_{i-1}]$

   Since all intended answers contain a subset of tuples of $V\langle U_i \rangle[ss_{i-1}]$, $Delta$, which is the sum of all actual answers, is also a subset of $V\langle U_i \rangle[ss_{i-1}]$.

3. There are insertions and deletions after U_i.

   Let t be a tuple in $Delta$. We want to show that either t should be in the view at state ss_i, or t will be removed from $Delta$ by the algorithm. The view at state ss_i is

$t \in MV[ws_{i-1}] \cup V\langle U_i\rangle[ss_{i-1}]$. Consider $BT(t)$, the set of tuples that actually derive t. There are three possible scenarios.

(A) All tuples in $BT(t)$ (except U_i) exist in source base relations at the source state ss_{i-1}. In this scenario, we have $t \in MV[ws_{i-1}] \cup V\langle U_i\rangle[ss_{i-1}]$, because at state ss_i, those tuples in $BT(t)$ together with U_i will derive t.

(B) There are one or more tuples in $BT(t)$ (except U_i) that do not exist in source base relations at source state ss_{i-1}. Those tuples must have been brought to $Delta$ because of insertions after U_i. Let the collection of those insertions be I. There are two subcases in this scenario:

  i. There exists at least one U_l in I such that U_l is not precede by a deletion of a tuple with the same projection attributes. In this case, when processing U_l in line 17, tuple t will be removed from $Delta$.

  ii. For all updates $U_l \in I$, there $\exists U_l' < U_l$ such that U_l' is a deletion and $\Pi_{proj}(U_l') = \Pi_{proj}(U_l)$. In this case, t should also be in $MV[ws_{i-1}] \cup V\langle U_i\rangle[ss_{i-1}]$. We can see this from the following argument. Let the first such deletion be U_l''. We know U_l'' derives t since it agrees on all projection attributes (as well as key attributes) with U_l. We also know that U_l'' exists in base relation at state ss_{i-1}. All those deleted tuples (such as U_l'' together with tuples in $BT(t)$ and U_i will derive t at source state ss_i.

This completes the proof for Case II(b).

Now that we have proved in Case II(a) that

$$V\langle U_i\rangle[ss_{i-1}] \subset Delta \implies V[ss_{i-1}] \cup V\langle U_i\rangle[ss_{i-1}] \subset V[ss_{i-1}] \cup Delta$$

Also we have proved in Case II(b) that

$$Delta \subset MV[ws_{i-1}] \cup V\langle U_i\rangle[ss_{i-1}]$$
$$\implies MV[ws_{i-1}] \cup Delta \subset MV[ws_{i-1}] \cup V\langle U_i\rangle[ss_{i-1}]$$

From inductive hypothesis $V[ss_{i-1}] = MV[ws_{i-1}]$, we can infer that $V[ss_{i-1}] \cup V\langle U_i\rangle[ss_{i-1}] = MV[ws_{i-1}] \cup Delta$. That is, we proved expression (B.1).

From Case I and II, we proved $MV[ws_i] = V[ss_i]$ for any update U_i. We established a one to one relationship between the sequence of warehouse states and a sequence of consistent source states, therefore, the C-Strobe algorithm is complete. ∎

Notes

1. Note incidentally that if modifications are treated as a delete-insert pair, then T-Strobe can process the pair within a single transaction, easily avoiding inconsistencies. However, for performance reasons we may still want to modify T-Strobe to handle modifications as a third type of action processed at the warehouse. As stated earlier, we do not describe this straightforward extension here.
2. After T_2 commits, its updates are sent separately from sources x and y. Therefore, one update necessarily arrives before the other; in this case, U_2 arrives from y before U_3 arrives from x.

References

1. R. Alonso, D. Barbara, and H. Garcia-Molina. Data caching issues in an information retrieval system. *ACM Transaction on Database Systems*, 15(3):359–384, September 1990.

2. E. Baralis, S. Ceri, and S Paraboschi. Conservative timestamp revised for materialized view maintenance in a data warehouse. In *Proceedings of the Workshop on Materialized Views, Techniques and Applications*, pages 1–9, Montreal, Canada, June 1996.

3. Y. Breitbart, H. Garcia-Molina, and A. Silberschatz. Overview of multidatabase transaction management. *VLDB Journal*, 1(2):181–239, October 1992.

4. P.A. Bernstein, V. Hadzilacos, and N. Goodman. *Concurrency Control and Recovery in Database Systems*. Addison-Wesley, Reading, Massachusetts, 1987.

5. J.A. Blakeley, P.-A. Larson, and F.W. Tompa. Efficiently updating materialized views. In *Proceedings of ACM SIGMOD Conference*, pages 61–71, Washington, D.C., June 1986.

6. M. Cochinwala and J. Bradley. A multidatabase system for tracking and retrieval of financial data. In *VLDB Conference*, pages 714–721, 1994.

7. L.S. Colby, T. Griffin, L. Libkin, I.S. Mumick, and H. Trickey. Algorithms for deferred view maintenance. In *Proceedings of ACM SIGMOD Conference*, pages 469–480, Montreal, Quebec, Canada, June 1996.

8. A. Courtney, W. Janssen, D. Severson, M. Spreitzer, and F. Wymore. Inter-language unification, release 1.5. Technical Report ISTL-CSA-94-01-01 (Xerox accession number P94-00058, Xerox PARC, May 1994.

9. S. Ceri and J. Widom. Deriving production rules for incremental view maintenance. In *VLDB Conference*, pages 577–589, Barcelona, Spain, September 1991.

10. Rob Goldring and Beth Hamel, January 1996. Personal correspondence about IBM's data warehouse customer needs.

11. A. Gupta and I.S. Mumick. Maintenance of materialized views: Problems, techniques, and applications. *IEEE Data Engineering Bulletin, Special Issue on Materialized Views and Data Warehousing*, 18(2):3–18, June 1995.

12. A. Gupta, I. Mumick, and V. Subrahmanian. Maintaining views incrementally. In *Proceedings of ACM SIGMOD Conference*, pages 157–166, Washington, D.C., May 1993.

13. H. Garcia-Molina and G. Wiederhold. Read-only transactions in a distributed database. *ACM Transaction on Database Systems*, 7(2):209–234, June 1982.

14. R. Gallersdorfer and M. Nicola. Improving performance in replicated databases through relaxed coherency. In *VLDB Conference*, pages 445–456, Zurich, Switzerland, September 1995.

15. A. Gupta and J. Widom. Local verification of global integrity constraints in distributed databases. In *Proceedings of ACM SIGMOD Conference*, pages 49–58, Washington, D.C., May 1993.

16. J.V. Harrison and S.W. Dietrich. Maintenance of materialized views in a deductive database: An update propagation approach. In *Proceedings of the 1992 JICLSP Workshop on Deductive Databases*, pages 56–65, 1992.

17. R. Hull and G. Zhou. A framework for supporting data integration using the materialized and virtual approaches. In *Proceedings of ACM SIGMOD Conference*, pages 481–492, Montreal, Quebec, Canada, June 1996.

18. W.H. Inmon and C. Kelley. *Rdb/VMS: Developing the Data Warehouse*. QED Publishing Group, Boston, Massachusetts, 1993.

19. W. Labio and H. Garcia-Molina. Efficient snapshot differential algorithms in data warehousing. In *VLDB Conference*, pages 63–74, September 1996.

20. B. Lindsay, L.M. Haas, C. Mohan, H. Pirahesh, and P. Wilms. A snapshot differential refresh algorithm. In *Proceedings of ACM SIGMOD Conference*, Washington, D.C., May 1986.

21. X. Qian and G. Wiederhold. Incremental recomputation of active relational expressions. *IEEE Transactions on Knowledge and Data Engineering*, 3(3):337–341, September 1991.

22. A. Segev and W. Fang. Currency-based updates to distributed materialized views. In *ICDE Conference*, pages 512–520, Los Alamitos, February 1990.

23. O. Shmueli and A. Itai. Maintenance of views. In *Proceedings of ACM SIGMOD Conference*, pages 240–255, Boston, Massachusetts, May 1984.

24. A. Segev and J. Park. Updating distributed materialized views. *IEEE Transactions on Knowledge and Data Engineering*, 1(2):173–184, June 1989.

25. Sybase, Inc. *Command Reference Manual*, release 4.9 edition, 1992.

26. J.L. Wiener, H. Gupta, W.J. Labio, Y. Zhuge, H. Garcia-Molina, and J. Widom. A system prototype for warehouse view maintenance. In *Proceedings of the Workshop on Materialized Views, Techniques and Applications*, pages 26–33, Montreal, Canada, June 1996.
27. G. Wiederhold and X. Qian. Consistency control of replicated data in federated databases. In *Proceedings of the IEEE Workshop on Management of Replicated Data*, pages 130–132, Houston, Texas, November 1990.
28. Y. Zhuge, H. Garcia-Molina, J. Hammer, and J. Widom. View maintenance in a warehousing environment. In *Proceedings of ACM SIGMOD Conference*, pages 316–327, San Jose, California, May 1995.
29. Y. Zhuge, J. L. Wiener, and H. Garcia-Molina. Multiple view consistency for data warehousing. In *ICDE Conference*, Birmingham, UK, April 1997.

Distributed and Parallel Databases, 6, 41–71 (1998)

Distributed Multi-Level Recovery
in Main-Memory Databases

RAJEEV RASTOGI   rastogi@research.bell-labs.com

PHILIP BOHANNON[*]   bohannon@research.bell-labs.com

JAMES PARKER   parker@research.bell-labs.com

AVI SILBERSCHATZ   avi@research.bell-labs.com
Bell Laboratories, 700 Mountain Ave., Murray Hill, NJ 07974

S. SESHADRI   seshad@cse.iitb.ernet.edu

S. SUDARSHAN   sudarsha@cse.iitb.ernet.edu
Indian Institute of Technology, Bombay, India

Recommended by: Jeffrey F. Naughton and Gerhard Weikum

Abstract. In this paper we present recovery techniques for *distributed main-memory* databases, specifically for client-server and shared-disk architectures. We present a recovery scheme for client-server architectures which is based on shipping log records to the server, and two recovery schemes for shared-disk architectures—one based on page shipping, and the other based on broadcasting of the log of updates. The schemes offer different tradeoffs, based on factors such as update rates.

Our techniques are extensions to a distributed-memory setting of a centralized recovery scheme for main-memory databases, which has been implemented in the Dalí main-memory database system. Our centralized as well as distributed-memory recovery schemes have several attractive features—they support an explicit multi-level recovery abstraction for high concurrency, reduce disk I/O by writing *only* redo log records to disk during normal processing, and use per-transaction redo and undo logs to reduce contention on the system log. Further, the techniques use a fuzzy checkpointing scheme that writes only dirty pages to disk, yet minimally interferes with normal processing—all but one of our recovery schemes do not require updaters to even acquire a latch before updating a page. Our log shipping/broadcasting schemes also support concurrent updates to the same page at different sites.

Keywords: distributed systems, transactions, logging, locking, concurrency control, recovery

1. Introduction

A large number of applications (e.g., call routing and switching in telecommunications, financial applications, automation control) require high performance access to data with response time requirements of the order of a few milliseconds to tens of milliseconds. Traditional disk-based database systems are incapable of meeting the high performance needs of such applications due to the latency of accessing data that is disk-resident. An attractive approach to providing applications with low (and predictable) response times is to load the entire database into main-memory. Databases for such applications are often of

---

[*] A Ph.D. candidate in the Department of Computer Science at Rutgers University.

the order of tens or hundreds of megabytes, which can easily be supported in main-memory. Further, machines with main memories of 8 gigabytes or more are already available, and with the falling price of RAM, machines with such large main memories will become cheaper and more common.

One approach for implementing such high performance databases is to provide a large buffer-cache to a traditional disk-based system. In contrast, in a *main-memory database system* (MMDB) (see, e.g., [7, 12, 9, 5]), the entire database can be directly mapped into the virtual address space of the process and locked in memory. Data can be accessed either directly by virtual memory pointers, or indirectly via location independent database offsets that can be quickly translated to memory addresses. During data access, there is no need to interact with a buffer manager, either for locating data, or for fetching/pinning buffer pages. Also, objects larger than the system's page size can be stored contiguously, thereby simplifying retrieval or in-place use. Thus, data access using a main-memory database is very fast compared to using disk-based storage managers, even when the disk-based manager has sufficient memory to cache all data pages.

Distributed architectures in which several machines are connected by a fast network, and perform database accesses and updates in parallel, provide significant further performance improvements for a number of applications. For example, consider applications in which transactions are predominantly read-only and update rates are low (e.g., number translation and call routing in telecommunications). Each machine can locally access data cached in memory, thus avoiding network communication which could be fairly expensive. Another example is Computer Aided Design applications, where locality of reference is very high, update transactions are long, and interactive response time is very important.

Distribution also enhances fault tolerance, which is required in many mission-critical applications, even if data fits easily in a single machine's main-memory. In this case, especially with low update rates, a distributed database is preferable to a hot-spare since the load can be distributed in the non-failure case leading to improved performance.

The recovery scheme used in the Dalí main-memory database system [9, 1] is based on the main-memory recovery scheme presented in [10]. The recovery scheme of [10] provides important features such as *transient undo logging* in which undo log records are kept in memory and only written to disk if required for checkpointing, per-transaction logs in memory to reduce contention on the system log tail, and recovery using only a single pass over the system log. The recovery scheme used in Dalí provides several further extensions, such as *multi-level recovery* ([20, 14, 13]), and *fuzzy checkpointing* [18, 8].

The goal of the work described here was to extend the Dalí recovery scheme to the distributed memory case, simultaneously maintaining the advantages of the single-site scheme, and efficiently supporting the applications described above. For example, we can make use of transient undo logging to reduce the size of the log written to disk, as well as the size of the log sent across network links in distributed protocols.

We present three distinct but related distributed recovery schemes – the first for *client-server* architectures, and the second and third for *shared disk* architectures. These are all "data-shipping" schemes (see, e.g., [6]) in which a transaction executes at a single site, fetching data (pages) as required from other sites. Distributed commit protocols are not needed as in "function-shipping" environments. While shared disk architectures have traditionally been closely tied to hardware platforms (e.g., VAXcluster), UNIX-based shared disk platforms and network of workstation architectures with similar performance characteristics are becoming more common.

A key property of the client-server scheme and one of the shared disk schemes is that concurrent updates are possible at granularities smaller than a page-size, thereby minimizing "false-sharing" (that is, apparent conflicts due to coarse-granularity locking) and consequently, needless network accesses to resolve false sharing. Our distributed recovery algorithms provide the advanced features of our centralized recovery algorithms, such as transient undo logging, explicit multi-level recovery, and fuzzy checkpointing. Site or global recovery requires only a single pass over the system log, starting from the end of the system log recorded in the most recent checkpoint.

The remainder of the paper is organized as follows. We present background on multi-level recovery and the single-site algorithm on which the present work is based in Section 2. Related work is presented in Section 3. We present our client-server recovery algorithm in Section 4. Section 5 describes our shared disk model, while Sections 6 and 7 present our shared disk recovery algorithms. Section 8 concludes the paper.

2. Overview of Main-Memory Recovery

In this section we present a review of multi-level recovery concepts and an overview of the single-site main-memory recovery scheme used in the Dalí system. Low-level details of our scheme are described in [2].

In our scheme, data is logically organized into *regions*. A region can be a tuple, an object, or an arbitrary data structure like a list or a tree. Each region has a single associated lock, referred to as the *region lock*, with exclusive (X) and shared (S) modes that guard updates and accesses to the region, respectively.

2.1. Multi-Level Recovery

Multi-level recovery [20, 14, 13] provides recovery support for enhanced concurrency based on the semantics of operations. Specifically, it permits the use of weaker *operation* locks in place of stronger shared/exclusive region locks.

A common example is index management, where holding physical region locks until transaction commit leads to unacceptably low levels of concurrency. If undo logging has been done physically (e.g. recording exactly which bytes were modified to insert a key into the index) then the transaction management system must ensure that these physical undo descriptions are valid until transaction commit. Since the descriptions refer to byte changes at specific positions, this typically implies that the region locks on the updated index nodes must be held until transaction commit to ensure correct *recovery*, in addition to considerations for concurrent access to the index.

The multi-level recovery approach is to replace these low-level physical undo log records with higher level logical undo log records containing undo descriptions at the operation level. Thus, for an insert operation, physical undo records would be replaced by a logical

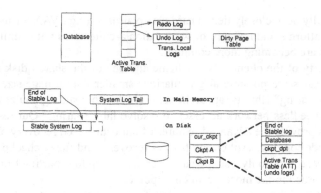

Figure 1. Overview of Recovery Structures

undo record indicating that the inserted key must be deleted. Once this replacement is made, the region locks may be released and only (less restrictive) operation locks need to be retained. For example, region locks on the particular nodes involved in an insert can be released, while an operation lock on the newly inserted key that prevents the key from being accessed or deleted is held.

2.2. System Overview

Figure 1 gives an overview of the structures used for recovery. The database (a sequence of fixed size pages) is mapped into the address space of each process and is in main memory, with (two) checkpoint images Ckpt_A and Ckpt_B on disk. Also stored on disk are 1) cur_ckpt, an "anchor" pointing to the most recent valid checkpoint image for the database, and 2) a single system log containing redo information, with its tail in memory. The variable end_of_stable_log stores a pointer into the system log such that all records prior to the pointer are known to have been flushed to the stable system log.

There is a single *active transaction table* (ATT) in main-memory which stores separate redo and undo logs for active transactions, in addition to information about transaction status. A dirty page table, dpt, is maintained in memory to record pages that have been updated since the last checkpoint. For simplicity of presentation, we assume that the dirty page table is maintained as a bitmap with one bit per page. The ATT (with undo logs, but without redo logs) and the dirty page table are also stored with each checkpoint image. The dirty page table in a checkpoint image is referred to as ckpt_dpt.

2.3. Transactions and Operations

Transactions, in our model, consist of a sequence of multi-level operations, similar to [13]. We briefly describe the model below. Each operation has a level L_i associated with it. An operation at level L_i can consist of a sequence of operations at level L_{i-1}. Transactions, assumed to be at level L_n, call operations at level L_{n-1}. Physical updates to regions are level L_0 operations. For transactions, we distinguish between *pre-commit*, when the commit record enters the system log in memory, establishing a point in the serialization order, and *commit* when the commit record hits the stable log. For operations, we use the terms commit and pre-commit interchangeably since both refer to the time when the commit record enters the system log in memory.

Each transaction obtains an *operation* lock before it executes an operation; the operation lock is granted if the operation commutes with other operation locks held by other active transactions. Level L_0 operations obtain region locks instead of operation locks. The locks on the region are released once the L_1 operation pre-commits; similarly, an operation lock at level L_i is held until the transaction or the containing operation (at level L_{i+1}) commits. All the locks acquired by a transaction are released once it commits.[1]

2.4. Logging Model

The recovery algorithm maintains separate *local* undo and redo logs in memory for each transaction. These are stored as a linked list off an entry for the transaction in the ATT. Each physical update (to a part of a region) generates physical undo and redo log records that are appended to the respective local log. When a transaction/operation pre-commits, the current contents of the transaction's local redo log are appended to the system log tail in memory, and the logical undo description for the operation is included in an operation commit log record appended to the system log. Thus, with the exception of logical undo descriptors, only redo records are written to the system log during normal processing.

Also, when an operation pre-commits, the undo log records for its suboperations/updates are replaced in the transaction's (local) undo log with a logical undo log record containing the undo description for the operation. In-memory undo logs of transactions that have committed are deleted since they are not required again.[2]

The system log is flushed to disk when a transaction commits. For each redo log record written to disk, pages touched by the update on the log record are marked dirty in the dirty page table, dpt, by the flushing procedure. In our single-site recovery scheme, update actions do not obtain latches on pages – instead region locks are obtained to ensure that updates do not interfere with each other.[3] Eliminating latching significantly decreases access costs in main-memory, and reduces programming complexity. Recovery related actions that are normally taken on page latching, such as setting of dirty bits for the page, are now performed based on log records written to the redo log. (Our distributed-memory schemes, with the exception of one of the shared-disk schemes, do not obtain page latches either; the sole exception uses page latching to ensure cache coherency, which is not a problem in the single-site case.) The redo log is used as a single unifying resource to coordinate the application's interaction with the recovery system, and this approach has proven very useful.

2.5. Ping-pong Checkpointing

Consistent with the terminology in main-memory database literature, we use the term *checkpoint* to mean a copy of the main-memory database which is stored on disk, and the term *checkpointing* to refer to the action of creating a checkpoint. This terminology differs slightly from the terminology used, for example, in ARIES [14].

Traditional recovery schemes implement *write-ahead logging* (WAL), whereby all undo logs for updates on a page are flushed to disk before the page is flushed to disk. In such systems, to guarantee the WAL property, typically a latch on a page is obtained, all log records pertaining to the page are flushed to stable storage, the page is copied to disk, and the latch released. Updaters also obtain the same page latch, thereby preventing concurrent updates while a page is being flushed to disk. As a result of not obtaining latches on pages during updates, it is not possible to enforce the write-ahead logging policy, since pages may be updated even as they are being written out.

Instead, our recovery algorithm makes use of a strategy called *ping-pong checkpointing* (see, e.g., [19]). In ping-pong checkpointing two copies of the database image are stored on disk, and alternate checkpoints write dirty pages to alternate copies. Writing alternate checkpoints to alternate copies permits a checkpoint that is being created to be temporarily inconsistent; i.e., updates may have been written out without corresponding undo records having been written. However, after writing out dirty pages, sufficient redo and undo log information is written out to bring the checkpoint to a consistent state. Even if a failure occurs while creating one checkpoint, the other checkpoint is still consistent and can be used for recovery.

Keeping two copies of a main-memory database on disk for ping-pong checkpointing does not have a very high space penalty, since disk space is much cheaper than main-memory. Further, ping-pong checkpointing has several other benefits. For instance, although many recovery schemes assume page writes are atomic, in reality they are not, and complex schemes are needed to detect and recover from incomplete page writes resulting from, for example, power failures. Incomplete page writes cause no problems with ping-pong checkpointing, since the previous checkpoint image is still available. Ping-pong checkpointing also permits some physical and logical consistency checks to be performed on the checkpoint before declaring it successfully completed.

Before writing any dirty data to disk, the checkpoint notes the current end of the stable log in the variable end_of_stable_log, which will be stored with the checkpoint. This is the start point for scanning the system log when recovering from a crash using this checkpoint. Next, the contents of the (in-memory) ckpt_dpt are set to those of the dpt and the dpt is zeroed (noting of end_of_stable_log and zeroing of dpt are done atomically with respect to flushing). The pages written out are the pages that were either dirty in the ckpt_dpt of the last completed checkpoint, or dirty in the current (in-memory) ckpt_dpt, or in both. In other words, all pages are written out that were modified since the current checkpoint image was previously written, namely, pages that were dirtied since the last-but-one checkpoint. This is necessary to ensure that updates described by log records preceding the current checkpoint's end_of_stable_log have made it in the database image in the current checkpoint.

Checkpoints write out dirty pages without obtaining any latches and thereby avoid interfering with normal operations. The checkpoint image is thus *fuzzy*. Fuzzy checkpointing however could result in two problems for recovery:

- the checkpoint page image may contain partial updates of an operation

- the undo log record for an update may not be in the stable system log (which could result in a problem if the system were to crash immediately after the checkpoint).

The first problem is solved by our policy of always writing physical redo log records. By applying physical redo log records (whose effects are idempotent) to a checkpoint page image we can ensure that we can obtain a page image that does not contain any partial updates.

The second problem is solved by ensuring that for any update whose effects have made it to the checkpoint image, one of the following holds: 1) corresponding physical undo log records are written out to disk after the database image has been written or 2) all physical redo log records for the operation (corresponding to the partial update) as well as the logical undo descriptor in the operation commit log record are on stable storage. This is performed by checkpointing the ATT and flushing the log after checkpointing the data. The checkpoint of the ATT writes out undo log records, as well some other status information. In case the operation containing the partial update completes and consequently the undo log records are removed from the ATT before the checkpoint of the ATT, the log flush ensures that all log records corresponding to the operation (containing the partial update) as well as the operation commit log record are on stable storage. The checkpoint is declared completed (and consistent) by toggling cur_ckpt to point to the new checkpoint.

2.6. Abort Processing

When a transaction aborts, that is, does not successfully complete execution, updates/operations described by log records in the transaction's undo log are undone by traversing the undo log backwards from the end. Transaction abort is carried out by executing, in reverse order, every undo record just as if the execution were part of the transaction.

Following the philosophy of *repeating history* [14], new physical redo log records are created for each physical undo record encountered during the abort. Similarly, for each logical undo record encountered, a new "compensation" or "proxy" operation is executed based on the undo description. Log records for updates performed by the operation are generated as during normal processing. Furthermore, when the proxy operation commits, all its undo log records are deleted along with the logical undo record for the operation that was undone. The commit record for the proxy operation serves a purpose similar to that served by *compensation log records* (CLRs) in ARIES – during restart recovery, when it is encountered, the logical undo log record for the operation that was undone is deleted from the transaction's undo log, thus preventing it from being undone again.

2.7. Recovery

Restart recovery begins by initializing the ATT and transaction undo logs to the ATT and undo logs stored in the most recent checkpoint, loads the database image and sets dpt to zero. Next, recovery processes redo log records. Recall that as part of the checkpoint operation, the end of the system log on disk, end_of_stable_log, is noted before the database image is checkpointed. This value of end_of_stable_log becomes the "begin recovery point" for the checkpoint once the checkpoint has completed. All updates described by log records preceding this point are guaranteed to be reflected in the checkpointed database image.

Thus, during restart recovery only redo log records following the end_of_stable_log for the last completed checkpoint of the database are applied. Restart recovery ignores redo log records for updates performed by an operation if the commit log record for the operation is not found in the system log. Such log records represent uncommitted updates, and may not have corresponding undo records in the checkpointed ATT. However, if the undo records are absent, the effects of the log records will not be reflected in the checkpointed database image. Such records would be present only due to a crash while the log records for an operation were being flushed.

During the application of redo log records, appropriate pages in dpt are set to dirty for each log record and necessary actions are taken to keep the checkpointed image of the ATT consistent with the log as it is applied. These actions on the ATT mirror the actions taken during normal processing. For example, when an operation commit log record is encountered, lower level log records in the transaction's undo log for the operation are replaced by a higher level undo description.

Once all the redo log records have been applied, the active transactions are rolled back. To do this, all completed operations that have been invoked directly by the transaction, or have been directly invoked by an incomplete operation, have to be rolled back. However, the order in which operations of different transactions are rolled back is very important, so that an undo at level L_i sees data structures that are consistent [13]. First, all operations (across all transactions) at L_0 that must be rolled back are rolled back, followed by all operations at level L_1, then L_2 and so on.

3. Connection to Related Work

Multi-level recovery and variants thereof, primarily for disk-based systems, have been proposed in the literature [20, 13, 14]. Like these schemes, our schemes repeat history, generate log records during undo processing and log operation commits when undo operations complete (similar to CLRs described in [14]). Also, as in [13], transaction rollback at crash recovery is performed level by level. Some of the features of our main-memory recovery technique which impact the distributed schemes are:

1. Due to transient undo logging, no physical undo logs are written out to the global log except during checkpoints.

2. Separate undo logs are maintained in memory for active transactions. A result is that transaction rollback does not need to access the global log, part of which could be on disk.

3. Our single-site scheme does not require latching of pages during updates, which is inconvenient and expensive in either a main-memory DB or an OODB setting. Actions that are normally taken on page latching, such as setting of dirty bits for the page, are efficiently performed based on physical redo log records written to the global log. (One of our shared-disk schemes uses page latching for ensuring cache consistency, while the other shared-disk scheme does not.)

4. The correctness requirements of the *write-ahead logging* policy are accomplished with a single flush for the entire database during a checkpoint, rather than (potentially) one flush per page.

5. Our scheme does not perform in-place update of the disk image during page flush, instead using ping-pong checkpointing.

In the ARIES-SD [15] family of schemes for recovery in the shared disk environment, each site maintains a separate log, and pages are shipped between sites. Our shared-disk log-shipping scheme does not ship pages, but instead broadcasts log records, taking advantage of cheap application of these log records in main-memory, and permitting *concurrent updates* at a smaller-than-page granularity. In our shared disk schemes, log flushes are driven by the release of a lock from a site, in order to support repeating of history and correct rollback of multi-level actions during crash recovery. The "super fast" method of ARIES-SD [15] does not describe flushes to protect the early release of locks, making it unclear how that scheme supports logical undo and high-concurrency index operations.

In [17], the authors propose recovery schemes for the shared disk environment which assume page-level concurrency control and the NO-STEAL page write policy — neither of which are assumptions made in our schemes.

In [16], the authors show how the ARIES recovery algorithm described in [14] can be extended to a client-server environment. In contrast to our client-server scheme, their scheme involves the clients as well as the server in the checkpointing process. We also support concurrent updates to a page by different clients, which is not supported in [16].

In [4], object-level as well as adaptive locking and replica management are discussed, but recovery considerations are not extensively addressed. In [6], the client-server recovery scheme for the Exodus storage manager (ESM-CS) is described. This recovery scheme, based on ARIES [14], requires page-level locking until end of transaction (for example, the Commit Dirty Page List).

4. Client-Server Recovery Scheme

In this section, we describe the client-server recovery scheme. Our system model is as follows.

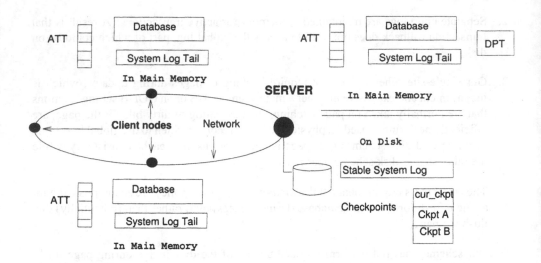

Figure 2. Client-Server Architecture

- There is a single server with stable storage, which is responsible for co-ordinating all the logging, and for performing checkpoints and recovery (see Figure 2). The server maintains a copy of the entire database in memory.

- Multiple clients may be connected to the server; each client has a copy of the entire database in its memory.

- A transaction executes at a single client and updates/accesses the copy of the database at the client.

- The network is FIFO and reliable.

As a result of updating the local copy of the database, database pages updated by a client may not be *current* at some other client. Therefore, a page at a client is in one of two states – *valid* or *invalid*. Invalid pages contain stale versions of certain data due to updates by other clients and are refreshed by obtaining the latest copy of the page from the server.

Transactions follow the *callback locking* scheme [11, 4] when obtaining and releasing locks. Each client site has a *local lock manager* (LLM) which caches locks and a *global lock manager* (GLM) at the server keeps track of locks cached at the various clients. Transaction requests for locks cached locally are handled at the client itself. However, requests for locks not cached locally are forwarded to the GLM which *calls back* the lock from other clients that may have cached the lock in a conflicting mode (before granting the lock request). A client relinquishes a lock in response to a callback as soon as transactions currently holding the lock (if any) release the lock.

The server maintains the **dpt** and the ATT (for all transactions in the client-server system) while the clients maintain the ATT for the transactions belonging to that client. The log records for updates generated by a transaction at a client site are stored in that site's ATT.

Client sites do not maintain a system log on disk, but keep a system log tail in memory and append log records from the local redo logs to this tail when operations commit/abort. Checkpointing is performed solely at the server, and follows the same procedure as the centralized case.

When a lock is relinquished from a site or a transaction commits, log records in the system log are shipped by the client to the server. In the case of transaction commit, the client waits for the server to flush the newly received log records to disk before reporting the commit to the user. The shipped redo log records are used to update the server's copy of the affected pages, ensuring that pages shipped to clients from the server are current (note that pages are shipped only from the server to clients and never vice versa). This enables our scheme to support concurrent updates to a single page at multiple clients since re-applying the updates at the server causes them to be merged (this approach is also adopted in [3]). Shipping the log records will usually be cheaper than shipping pages, and the cost of applying the log records themselves is small since, in our main-memory database context, the server will not have to read the affected pages from disk.

We will now describe our scheme in detail and also outline several possible optimizations to the basic ideas discussed above.

4.1. Basic Operations

We now describe the features which distinguish the client-server scheme from the centralized case, in terms of actions performed at the client and the server at specific points in processing.

- **Page Access:** In case a client accesses a page that is valid, it simply goes ahead without communicating with the server. Else, if the page is *invalid* (certain data on the page may be stale), then the client refreshes the page by 1) obtaining the most recent version of the page from the server, and 2) applying to the newly received page any local updates which have not been sent to the server (this step merges local updates with updates from other sites). The client then marks the page as valid. The server keeps track of clients that have the page in a valid state.

  To prevent race conditions, the client does not send log records to the server after asking for a page and before receiving it.

  An optimization of the above is to check for validity of pages at the time of acquisition of region locks from the server rather than on every access; for this optimization to be used, the set of pages covered by the region lock must be known.

- **Operation/Transaction Commit:**   At the client, redo log records are moved to the system log, a commit record is appended, and appropriate actions are performed on the transaction's undo log in the ATT as described for the centralized case. In case of transaction commit, the log records in the system log are shipped to the server, and commit processing waits until the server has acknowledged that the log records have been flushed to disk.

  Finally, all the locks acquired by the operation/transaction are released locally. The local lock manager at the site may however continue to cache the locks locally.

- **Lock Release:** When a lock is relinquished by a client, all redo log records that were generated under this lock need to be shipped to the server. The server then applies these log records to its database image to ensure that another client that obtains the same lock gets a copy of the pages which contains the updates described by these log records. A simple way to ensure that all log records generated under the lock are shipped to the server is to flush the system log from the client to the server.

  An optimization to avoid flushing the system log each time is to store the end of the client system log with the lock (at the client) when a X mode region lock or an operation lock is released by a transaction. Thus, for any region lock, all redo log records in the system log affecting that region precede the point in the log stored with the lock. Similarly, for an operation lock, all log records relating to the operation (including operation commit) precede the point in the system log stored with the lock. This location in the log is client-site-specific.

  Before a client site relinquishes an X mode region lock or operation lock to the server due to call-back, it ships to the server at least the portion of the system log which precedes the log pointer stored with the lock. This ensures that the next lock will not be acquired on the region until the server's copy is up to date, and the history of the update is in place in the server's logs. For X mode region locks, this flush ensures repeating of history on regions, while for operation locks this flush ensures that the server receives the logical undo descriptors in the operation commit log records for the operation which released the locks. Thus, if the server aborts a transaction after a site failure, the abort of this operation will take place at the logical level of the locks still held for it at the server.

- **Log Record Processing:** At the server, for each physical redo log record (received from a client), the undo log record is generated by reading the current contents of the page at the server. The new log record is then appended to the undo log for this transaction in the server's ATT. Next the update described by the redo log record is applied, following which the log record is appended to the redo log for the transaction in the server's ATT. Operation/transaction commit log records received from the client are processed by performing the same actions as in the centralized case when the log records were generated. In addition, for operation commit, the logical undo descriptor is extracted from the commit log record and appended to the undo log for the transaction in the server's ATT. For transaction commit, the client whose transaction committed is notified after the log flush to disk succeeds.

  By applying all the physical updates described in the physical log records to its pages, the server ensures that it always contains the latest updates on regions for locks which have been released to it from the clients. The effect of the logging scheme, as far as data updates are concerned, is just as if the client transaction actually ran at the server site.

- **Transaction Abort/Site Failures:** If a client site decides to abort a transaction, it processes the abort (as in the centralized case) using the undo logs for the transaction in the client's ATT. If the client site itself fails, the server will abort transactions that were active at the client using undo logs for the transaction in it's ATT(since the client cannot commit without communicating with the server, in case of partition, a decision to abort is enforceable by the server). If the server fails, then the complete system is brought down, and restart recovery is performed at the server as described in Section 2.7.

- **Page Invalidation**

  We complete our client-server scheme by presenting two methods, invalidate-on-update, and invalidate-on-lock, for ensuring that data accessed by a client is up-to-date.

  All actions described so far are used in common by both methods. In particular, both methods follow the rule that all log records pertaining to updates made under a lock are flushed to the server before the lock is relinquished from the site. Since the server would have applied the log records to its copy of the data, this ensures that when the server grants a lock, it has the current version of all pages containing data covered by that lock. However, when a client acquires a lock, it is still possible that the copy of one or more pages involved in the region for which the lock was obtained are not up-to-date at the client.

  Both methods mark pages at the clients as invalid, to denote that some of the data on the page is out of date. Even if a page is marked invalid, some of the data in the page may still be up-to-date, for instance, if the client has a region lock on the data. The first method, invalidate-on-update, is an eager method that marks pages as invalid at clients as soon as an update occurs at the server, while the second, invalidate-on-lock, is a more lazy method, marking pages as invalid at clients when the client gets a lock. The second scheme reduces invalidation messages by keeping extra per-lock information at the server. Details of the two methods are presented in Sections 4.2 and 4.3 respectively.

4.2. Invalidate-On-Update

The invalidate-on-update scheme works as follows. When the server receives log records from a client, it does the following. For each page that it updates, it sends *invalidate* messages to clients (other than the client that updated the page) that may have the page marked as valid. For all clients other than the client that updated the page, the server notes that the client does not have the page marked valid. Clients, on receiving the invalidate message, mark their page as invalid. Thus invalidation messages are received by clients before they can acquire a region lock on the updated data, and begin accessing the data.

Although the method is very simple and easy to implement, it has some drawbacks. For example, consider two sites s_1 and s_2 updating the same page concurrently under two different region locks. Let s_1 be the site that flushes its updates to the server first; the update will cause the server to send an invalidate message to s_2, which will then re-read the page from the server. However, if site s_2 accesses the page again *under the lock that it already has*, then the invalidate was not necessary, since the data in the region it has locked has not changed. The invalidate-on-lock scheme in the next section takes advantage of this observation to reduce overheads.

4.3. Invalidate-On-Lock

The invalidate-on-lock scheme decreases unnecessary invalidations and the overhead of sending invalidation messages by marking pages as invalid only when a lock on a region covering the page is obtained by a client. As a result, if two clients are updating different regions on the same page, as in the earlier example, no invalidation messages are sent to either client. By piggy-backing invalidation messages for updated pages on lock grant messages from the server, the overhead of sending separate invalidation messages in the previous scheme is eliminated.

The biggest benefit of the invalidate-on-lock scheme, however, is that there is no need to check for validity of a page on every access or update to the page—it suffices to check for validity at lock acquisition time.

To achieve the above, the scheme must associate with the lock for a region information about updates to that region. Specifically, when updates described by a physical redo record are applied to pages at the server, the updated pages are associated with the lock for the updated region. Thus, the scheme requires that it be possible to determine the region lock from the redo record. A simple way of obtaining this information is to require that an update call must specify not only the data to be updated, but also the region lock that protects the data. It is easy for a programmer to provide this information, since all updates must be made holding a region lock. The lock name can then be sent with the redo log record.

This scheme also requires that the server associate a *Log Sequence Number* (LSN), with each log record, which reflects both the order in which the record was applied to the server's copy of the page and the order in which it was added to the system log. For each page, the server stores the LSN of the most recent log record that updated the page, and the identity of the client which issued it. In addition, for each client, the server maintains in a *client page table* (cpt), the state of the page at the client (valid/invalid), along with the LSN for the page when it was last shipped to the client.

The server also maintains for each region lock a list of pages that are dirty due to updates to the region. For each page in the list, the server stores the LSN of the most recent log record received by the server that recorded an update to the part of the region on this page, and the client which performed the update. Thus, when a client is granted a region lock, if, for a page in the lock list, the LSN is greater than the LSN for the page when it was last shipped to the client, then the client page contains stale data for the region and must be invalidated.

The LSN information serves to minimize the shipping of pages to clients, marking a page as invalid only if there is an update performed under the region lock requested by the client, and the update has not yet been propagated to the client.

The additional actions for this scheme are as follows:

- **Log apply:** When the server applies to a page P a redo log record, LR, generated at client C under region lock L, it takes the following actions (after P has been updated). First, the LSN for P is set to the LSN for LR. Second, the entry for P in the list of dirty pages for L is updated (or created), setting the client to C, and the LSN to the LSN for LR.

- **Lock grant:** A set of invalidate messages is passed back to the client with the lock acquisition. The invalidate messages are for pages in the list associated with the lock being acquired that meet three criteria: 1) the page is cached at the client in the valid state, 2) the LSN of the page in the cpt for the client is smaller than the LSN of the page in the lock list, and 3) the client acquiring the lock was not the last to update the page under this lock. The invalidated pages are marked invalid in the cpt for the client and at the client site.

- **Page refresh:** When the server sends a page to a client (page refresh), at the server, the page is marked valid in the cpt for the client and the LSN for the page in the cpt is updated to be the LSN for the page at the server.

- **Lock list cleanup:** We are interested in keeping the list of pages with every lock as small as possible. This can be achieved by periodically deleting pages P from the list of lock L such that the following condition holds, where C is the client noted in the list of pages for L as the last client to update P:

  > Every client other than C has the page cached either in an invalid state or with LSN greater than or equal to the LSN for the page in the list for lock L.

The rationale for this rule is that the purpose of region lock lists is to determine pages that must be invalidated. However, if for a page in a client's cpt, the LSN is greater than the LSN for the page in the lock list, then the client has the most recent update to the region on the page, and thus the page will not need to be part of any invalidation list sent to the client.

5. Shared Disk Recovery: Model and Common Structures

In the shared disk approach, a number of machines are interconnected and also have direct access to disks over a fast network. The shared disk environment is used in many systems, such as the DEC VAXclusters, and provides benefits over a shared nothing architecture, such as faster access to non-local disks and fault-tolerance. Also, the basic advantage of shared disk schemes over the client-server schemes is that the algorithms are symmetric with respect to which site executes them, preventing one system from becoming a bottleneck in the system. As in our client-server scheme, in addition to careful consideration of the interaction with multi-level recovery, our main concern is minimizing false sharing through fine-grained concurrency control. This allows, for example, read-only transactions with a fully cached working set to proceed at main-memory speeds, an important property for our intended applications.

We now describe our shared disk recovery model.

- Each site maintains its own copy of the entire database in memory and its own system log on disk. Thus, there may be multiple logs in the system.

- Sites obtain locks from a *Global Lock Manager* (GLM); the function of the lock manager could be distributed for speed and reliability, but this is orthogonal to our discussion.

- Sites cache locks, and relinquish locks based on the *call back* locking mechanism described in Section 4. We assume the network is FIFO and reliable.

- Each site has its own system log on disk and therefore the logs are distributed. To repeat history during restart recovery, we need some mechanism to temporally order log records that affect the same region. To enable this, each site maintains a global timestamp counter TS_ctr, and a timestamp obtained from this counter is stored in each physical redo log record for an update. We will see the details of how this TS_ctr is maintained and used later.

- Each site maintains its own version of the *dirty page table* dpt, system log (a stable portion on disk *and* a tail in memory), and an ATT which stores information relating to transactions that execute at that site (with separate undo and redo log records for each transaction).

- A single pair of checkpointed images is maintained on disk for the database. A checkpoint image consists of an image of the database, the dirty page table ckpt_dpt, and for every site:

    1. end_of_stable_log – the point in the site's system log from which the system log must be scanned during recovery.
    2. a copy of the ATT at the site (containing undo logs).

In the next two sections, we present two schemes for shared disk concurrency control and recovery. The first is a page-shipping approach which is similar in spirit to the Invalidate-on-Update client-server mode. The second is a log shipping scheme which allows concurrent use of non-overlapping regions on a page across sites.

6. Page-Shipping Shared Disk Recovery Scheme

Our page-shipping scheme is similar in spirit to the Invalidate-on-Update client-server scheme in that a transaction at a site updating a region on a page is guaranteed to have the latest copy of the page. Therefore, concurrent updates to different regions of a page are not possible in this scheme.

6.1. Data Structures

We now describe data structures specific to the page-shipping scheme. Common data structures were described in Section 5. An overview of the data structures for this scheme is given in Figure 3.

In addition to the TS_ctr for the site, a timestamp for each page is maintained at each site in the *page timestamp table*, ptt, which keeps track of the TS_ctr value when the page was last updated. Each page has an associated *page* lock which helps in ensuring that a transaction always has the latest copy of the page while accessing or updating the page.

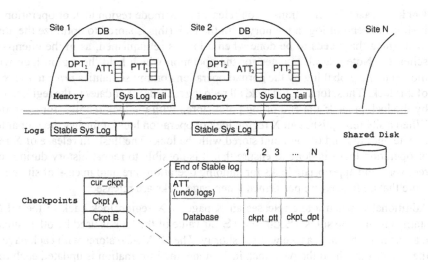

Figure 3. Page-Shipping Shared Disk Architecture

Sites cache locks, and relinquish locks based on the *call back* locking mechanism described earlier. Along with each of the two checkpoint images of the database is stored a checkpoint page timestamp table, referred to as ckpt_ptt.

6.2. Normal Processing

We describe below the actions taken during normal processing, in addition to those performed in the centralized case, to support distributed concurrency control and recovery. Checkpointing and recovery from system and site failure are described in subsequent subsections.

- **Update:** Like in the centralized case, before accessing a region, each transaction obtains a region lock from the LLM. Additional page locks are acquired in S(X) mode while accessing (updating) data on a page. If this lock is not cached at the site, actions are performed as described below under **Lock Acquisition**.

  Page locks for an access are released by a transaction once the access is completed; page locks for an update are released by a transaction only after the update on the page is completed. The value of TS_ctr at the site when the redo log record was generated is stored in the redo log record corresponding to the update. Also, the timestamp for the updated page (in the ptt) at the site is set to the TS_ctr stored in the log record.

  An important point to note is that log records in the system log may not be ordered on their TS_ctr values. This is because the value of TS_ctr is stored in the redo log record when the update is performed, but the log record is appended to the transaction local log, which is not flushed to the system redo log until operation or transaction commit.

- **Lock Release:** When a transaction releases an X mode region lock or operation lock, it stores the end of log in memory with the lock (this is stored to optimize the amount of flushing that needs to be done when a lock is relinquished, as in the client-server scheme). Note that all updates for the operation which held the region lock will be moved to the global log by the normal operation commit semantics *prior* to the release of this lock. Thus, for a region lock, all redo log records for updates to the region covered by the lock precede the end of log point stored with the lock (similar for operations). When a site relinquishes an X region lock or operation lock, it flushes the global log at its site until the end of log point stored with the lock. The flush on release of X region or operation locks is done to ensure that it is possible to repeat history during restart recovery, and appropriate locks for undoing operations are held in case of site crashes. Note that no flushes are performed when page locks are released.

  Additionally, when a site releases an X page or X region lock back to the GLM, it stamps it with the site's TS_ctr; the TS_ctr value of the lock is used by other sites that later acquire the lock, as we will see shortly. The GLM also stores with each page lock the site that last held the page lock in X mode; the information is updated each time a site relinquishes an X mode page lock,

- **Lock Acquisition:**

  A transaction acquiring a lock cached by the LLM need take no special action. If it is a page lock, then the page is already current at this site.

  When an X-mode page or region lock arrives from the GLM, it includes the timestamp from the last site that held the lock in X mode, as described above. Upon receiving an X region lock or page lock at a site, the site's TS_ctr is set to the maximum of 1) it's current value, and 2) the TS_ctr value associated with the incoming lock plus one.

  When a site acquires a page lock on behalf of a transaction from the GLM (that is, the lock is not already cached at the site), the site requests the page from the last site that held the page lock in X mode (using the site identifier sent with the lock). In order to handle single-site recovery, failure of the acquiring site to obtain a copy of the page, due to a failure of the site from which it is being requested, causes the lock acquisition to fail and the lock to be returned to the GLM unchanged.

Shipping timestamps with page locks ensures that log records for successive updates to a page at different sites are assigned increasing timestamp values. Shipping timestamps with region locks ensures that log records generated under conflicting locks are applied in the correct order during recovery even though redo log records in the individual site may not be ordered by timestamp (as mentioned earlier). However, the algorithm still works correctly, as shown in the discussion of recovery and correctness below.

6.3. Checkpointing

Unlike the centralized and client-server scheme, checkpointing in the shared disk environment requires coordination among the various sites. As mentioned above, a single pair of checkpointed images is maintained for all the sites.

The site initiating the checkpoint coordinates the operation, which consists of the following three steps at each site – 1) writing the database file image 2) writing the ATT and 3) flushing the global log. Below, we describe each step:

1. The coordinator announces the beginning of the checkpoint, at which time all sites (including the coordinator) note their current end_of_stable_log values, then make a copy of their dpts and zero their dpts. Note that zeroing the dpt and recording end_of_stable_log is done atomically with respect to flushes.

    Each site then makes a copy of its current ptt and sends it to the coordinator along with the end_of_stable_log (noted above), and a copy of the dpt. The coordinator constructs ckpt_dpt by or'ing together the copy of its dpt and all the dpts received from other sites (recall that we are assuming the dpt is a bitmap). The database pages to be written out during the checkpoint are the pages that are dirty in ckpt_dpt or in the ckpt_dpt in the previous checkpoint.

    For each page to be written out, the coordinator uses the ptts sent to it by the other sites and its own ptt to determine the site whose ptt contains the highest timestamp for the page. This site is responsible for writing the page to the checkpoint image. Once the coordinator has partitioned the set of pages to be written out among the various sites, each site is sent the set of page identifiers assigned to it. A site, upon receiving its assigned set of pages to write, proceeds to write those pages to the checkpoint image. Since no two sites will be assigned the same page, site can write pages concurrently.

    The coordinator then constructs ckpt_ptt by first reading the ckpt_ptt in the previous checkpoint into memory. For every page that was determined to be written out (by some site i), the timestamp for the page in ckpt_ptt is set to its timestamp in the copy of the ptt for site i. Finally, ckpt_dpt constructed earlier, ckpt_ptt and the end_of_stable_logs for all the sites are written to the checkpoint.

    Note that since the site with the highest timestamp for a page writes the page to the checkpoint image, updates to the page by log records preceding end_of_stable_log recorded for a site, are contained in the checkpoint. Furthermore, as will be discussed in the correctness section below, updates for a page recorded in log records with timestamps less than the timestamp for the page in ckpt_ptt are also contained in the checkpoint.

2. Once every site has written out the database image and reported this to the coordinator, the coordinator instructs each site to write out its ATT. Note that multiple sites can be concurrently writing out the ATT.

3. After writing out the ATT, each site flushes the global log at that site as in the centralized case. Finally, the database checkpoint is committed after all sites have completed their flushing.

6.4. Recovery

In case the entire system fails, *restart recovery* is performed by any one site, say j. The site j, which we will call the *acting coordinator* site, reads the following from the most recent checkpoint image: the database image, the ckpt_ptt, and for each site, the ATT and the end_of_stable_log. A separate page table ptt is initialized to ckpt_ptt and for each site i a separate dpt, dpt_i is initialized to contain zero bits for all pages. Starting from the end_of_stable_log point stored for a site in the checkpoint, the log records in all the system logs are merged as described below, and applied to the database. To merge the system logs, they are scanned in parallel; at each point, if the next log record in any of the system logs is not a redo log record, then any one such record is processed and the ATT for its site is modified as described for the centralized case in Section 2.7. On the other hand, if the next records in all the system logs are redo log records, then the log record output next is the one amongst them with the lowest timestamp value. If, for a page updated by the log record, the timestamp in the log record is greater than or equal to the timestamp for the page in ckpt_ptt, then 1) the update is applied to the page, 2) the page is marked dirty in the dpt for the site whose system log contains the record, and 3) the timestamp for the page in ptt is set to the maximum of its current value and the timestamp in the log record.

Note that redo records in the system log for a site may not be in timestamp order as mentioned earlier. However, this does not cause a problem and conflicting log records are applied in the order in which they were generated. The reason for this is that for two conflicting log records in separate system logs, the earlier log record and log records preceding it in its system log have lower timestamps than the log record generated later. This fact is revisited below in our overview of correctness.

Once the last log record has been processed, TS_ctr at the acting coordinator site j is set to the largest timestamp contained in the ptt at site j. Site j then rolls back in-progress operations in the ATTs for the various sites beginning with level L_0 and then considering successive levels L_1, L_2 and so on (as described in Section 2.7). When an operation in an ATT entry for a site i is being processed, actions are performed on the undo and redo logs for the entry. Furthermore, each redo log record generated when processing an operation for site i is assigned a timestamp equal to TS_ctr at site j, and when an operation pre-commits/aborts, log records from the redo log are appended to the system log for site i.

Next, site j flushes every site's system logs causing appropriate pages in the dpt for the site (maintained at site j) to be marked dirty. After this point, the other sites are involved in recovery. The TS_ctr at every site is set to the TS_ctr at site j after incrementing it by one. The dpt at each site is then set to the dpt maintained for the site during recovery at site j, and the database image and ptt at each site is set equal to the database image and ptt at site j. Finally ckpt_ptt and dpt for other sites are deleted from site j, bringing recovery to completion.

6.5. Overview of Correctness

In this section, we present additional arguments about the correctness of our page-shipping recovery scheme by discussing below several properties on which the correctness is based.

1. A page, i, in a checkpoint image reflects all updates with timestamp less than ckpt_ptt[i].

2. Any log record affecting page i prior to end_of_stable_log at any site has timestamp less than or equal to ckpt_ptt[i] and is reflected in the checkpoint image of page i.

3. If L_1 and L_2 are conflicting log records and L_1 is generated before L_2, then if L_2 is flushed to the stable log, then so is L_1.

4. If L_1 and L_2 are conflicting log records in different system logs and L_1 is generated before L_2, then L_1 and all log records preceding it in its system log have lower timestamps than L_2.

(1) follows from the fact that timestamps for pages in the ptt are set only after they are updated, and passing timestamps with page locks guarantees that successive updates to a page have non-decreasing timestamps (and in turn, assign non-decreasing timestamps to the ptt entry).

(2) For a log record that updates page i prior to end_of_stable_log at a site, (a) ppt[i] at the site is greater than or equal to the timestamp in the log record, (b) the page is in the dpt of the site and (c) the page at the site contains the update (when the site sends its ppt and dpt to the coordinator during the first phase of the checkpoint). Thus, since the site for which ppt[i] is the largest writes the page to the checkpoint image, ckpt_ppt[i] is greater than or equal to the timestamp in the log record. Also, since versions of a page with higher timestamps contain all updates in versions with lower timestamps, the update by the log record is reflected in the checkpoint image of page i.

(3) When the region lock covering L_1 was released, it must have followed the commit of an operation due to the rules of multi-level recovery. Thus, that log record would be moved to the global log during the operation commit, and would thus be before the point noted on release of the region lock. The flush to that point carried out when a region lock is released by a site guarantees the property.

(4) The shipping of TS_ctrs with region locks ensures this property. The reason for this is that L_1 is appended to the system log at its site before the X region lock for the updated region is released by the site. The timestamp assigned to the lock is the TS_ctr at the site for L_1 which is at least as large as the timestamps in L_1 and all the redo records preceding L_1 in the releasing site's system log. Before L_2 can be generated, its site has to acquire the region lock in X mode which causes the timestamp at the site where L_2 is generated to be set higher than the timestamp for the lock. Thus, L_2 is assigned a timestamp greater than L_1 as well as all log records preceding L_1.

Properties (1) through (4) can be used to show that our recovery scheme repeats history when scanning the system logs. Property (1) implies that updates to a page i by a log record do not need to be applied if ckpt_ptt[i] is greater than the timestamp in the log record. From property (2), it follows that log records preceding end_of_stable_log can be ignored since these updates are already contained in the checkpoint image. Property (3) ensures that log records in the system logs accurately and completely describe the history of updates to every region. Finally, property (4) ensures that conflicting updates described by log records that appear after end_of_stable_log are applied during recovery in the order in which they were performed during normal processing (in spite of timestamps possibly being out of order within a single site's log). Note that, for conflicting log records L_1 and L_2 on page i, L_1 generated before L_2, L_2 may precede end_of_stable_log for its site, while L_1 follows end_of_stable_log for its site. In this case, due to property (2), ckpt_ptt[i] would be greater than or equal to the timestamp for L_2 and the timestamp for L_2 would be greater than that for L_1. Thus, the update to page i by L_1 would not be applied during recovery.

6.6. Recovery from Site Failure

Our recovery algorithm can also be extended to deal with a site failure *without* performing a complete system restart, so long as the GLM data has not been lost, or can be regenerated from the other sites. If this is not the case, a full system recovery is performed instead.

Recovery from a single site failure is complicated since log records for updates by active transactions at the failed site may not have made it to stable storage while the updates themselves may have been propagated to other sites when the pages containing the updates are shipped between sites. There is no way to undo these updates since the undo information for them is contained is main-memory and is lost when the site failed. Thus, the only way to roll back the above set of updates is to recover the set of pages that the updates span. (Note that such a problem would not arise with a scheme providing lower concurrency, such as page locks held to end of transaction.)

In order to support this roll-back, it must be possible to associate with any region or operation lock the set of pages such that some part of the page may be updated by an operation that holds the lock; we call this set of pages as the pages *affected* by the lock.

The first step, when a site j recovers, is to determine the set of pages that must be recovered—these are pages that either:

1. May contain updates by uncommitted transactions from site j, or

2. Were last updated by site j.

The pages in (1) are those affected by any operation or X mode region lock held by site j at the GLM. The pages in (2) are those pages on which site j was the last site to have obtained an X page lock. The pages in (2) that are not in (1) are the set of pages that contain updates belonging to transactions that committed at site j. Note that for these pages, if a different site k holds an S lock on the page, the page need not be recovered, and the GLM merely notes that the site k has the latest version of the page.

Once the set of pages to be recovered are determined as described above, they are all locked in X mode by site j so that all updates to these pages by other sites are blocked (any other page locks held by site j are released).

Site j then retrieves from the most recent checkpoint, the database image, the ATT for site j, ckpt_ptt and the end_of_stable_log for each site. It then requests from every other site, the current end_of_stable_log at the site and the sequence of redo records in memory at the site (that is, redo records in the transaction local logs or in the system log after end_of_stable_log) involving updates to the pages being recovered. The redo pass is performed by scanning all the system logs as described in the Section 6.4 except that 1) only updates to pages being recovered are applied depending on the timestamps for these pages in ckpt_ptt, and the timestamps for only these updated pages are modified in ptt, 2) only the pages in the dpt for site j are marked dirty, 3) only actions on the ATT for site j are performed, and 4) the system log for a site is scanned until the end_of_stable_log returned by that site at the beginning of this recovery. After this, the in-memory redo records received from the various sites are applied in timestamp order to the pages being recovered, and the timestamps for the updated pages in ptt are set to the timestamp in the log record.

At the end of the redo pass, the pages being recovered contain updates by transactions at every other site and updates by transactions at site j for which log records are contained in the stable log (thus, updates described by redo log records in memory of site j when it crashed are absent – this includes the transaction local logs and the portion of the global log in main memory). At this point, other sites can be granted page locks held by site j if they request it. TS_ctr at site j is set to be greater than the largest timestamp in the ptt at site j.

Before rolling back in-progress operations, the locks that were cached at site j at the time it crashed are obtained by the recovery process at site j by consulting the GLM. As described in Section 2.7, rollback is performed level by level, with additional locks requested as is done during normal processing (see Section 7.2). Level L_i operation locks at site j can be released once all active operations at level L_{i+1} have been rolled back.

As in normal processing, TS_ctr at site j is incremented when a new lock is obtained, TS_ctr stored in a redo log record and in the timestamp entries for updated pages when the redo log is generated, and log flushes are performed when operation/X mode region locks are released by site j.

7. Log-Shipping Shared Disk Recovery Scheme

We are interested in improving the concurrency of the page-shipping shared disk recovery scheme by allowing multiple concurrent readers and writers of the same page at different sites, as long as the parts of the page they update come under different region locks. A result of this is that copies of a page at different sites may contain a different set of updates, which must be merged before the page is written to disk. Unlike the client-server case, there is no server to carry out the task of merging updates.

To solve the above problem, in our scheme, log records generated at a site are broadcast to all other sites, so the updates can be carried out there. Since log records are shipped, there is no need to ship pages. The scheme ensures that every time a site obtains a region lock, the most recent version of the region is guaranteed to be accessed at the site. More precisely, it guarantees that every time a site obtains any lock (whether an operation lock or a region lock), all log records generated by all operations which held the same lock in a conflicting mode have been applied to the local page images.

The idea of broadcasting log records leads to an architecture that essentially implements distributed shared memory, without the overhead of shipping pages. Note that the overhead of broadcasting log records to all the sites may not be too severe if update rates are not too high. Broadcasting may also be seen as a strategy to propagate updates early, possibly using greater bandwidth, but avoiding the latency of waiting for pages to be shipped when another transaction needs to update the data. Also, in some network architectures (e.g., ethernet), the cost of a broadcast to all sites may not be very different from the cost of sending a message to a single site.

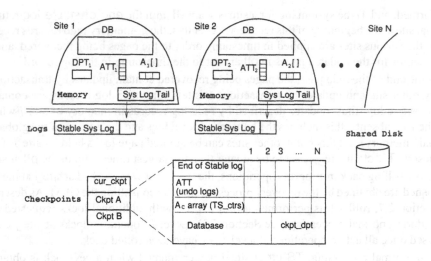

Figure 4. Log-Ship Shared Disk Architecture

7.1. Data Structures

An overview of data structures used for our shared disk scheme is given in Figure 4. In addition to the common elements described in Section 5, the log-based scheme maintains the following additional data structures. At every site j, an array of TS_ctrs (one TS_ctr per site), A_j is maintained in memory. $A_j[i]$ stores the timestamp of the latest update from site i that has been applied to the database at site j. A_j serves a purpose similar to ptts in the page-shipping scheme — it keeps track of the state of the database relative to log records.

With each checkpointed image on disk, each site stores the TS_ctr following which redo log records from that site must be applied to the database. Collectively these counters are referred to as A_C. Note that since pages are not shipped between sites, the log-shipping scheme does not need page locks.

7.2. Normal Processing

We describe below the actions taken during normal processing to support distributed concurrency control and recovery (in addition to those for the centralized case). Checkpointing and recovery from system and site failure are described in subsequent sections.

- **Log Records:** Every time a physical redo log record is moved from a transaction's local redo log to the system log, TS_ctr is incremented by 1 and stored in the log record. The timestamps are used to order log records that describe conflicting updates.

- **System Log Flush:** When the system log at site i is flushed to stable storage, each redo log record which has hit the disk is also broadcast to the other sites. The sending site i, also sets $A_i[i]$ to the timestamp in the log record. Flushing of a sequence of log records is completed once every log record has been written to disk as well as sent to the remaining sites. Also, as in the centralized case, pages updated by the flushed log records are marked dirty in the site's dpt.

- **Log Record Receipt:** A site j processes an update broadcast to it from site i as follows (updates are processed in the order in which they are received). On receiving a broadcast log record, the site applies the update to its local copy of the affected page(s), and sets the appropriate bits in its dpt. After updating the appropriate pages, the site sets $A_j[i]$ to the timestamp contained in the update (redo log record).

- **Lock Release:** The lock managers aid the scheme in two ways. First, as in the previous schemes, the current local end-of-log is noted with region and operation locks when the lock is released by a transaction, and the LLM ensures that the log is flushed to this point before releasing the lock from the site. This aids in recovery by ensuring that history is repeated, and when lower level locks are released, the logical undo actions which accompany the higher level locks have made it to disk. Since logs are broadcast on flush, it helps ensure that another site will receive the necessary log records before getting the same lock in a conflicting mode.

  Note that the FIFO property of the network does not ensure that a site j receives an update broadcast from a site i before it obtains the region lock for the updated region from the GLM (relinquished to the GLM by site i). In order to ensure that all previous updates to a region are received by a site before it obtains the region lock, the LLM before releasing a region lock from a site must ensure that not only have all redo log records preceding the end-of-log (noted for the lock) flushed to disk, but also that acknowledgments of receipt of the broadcast records have been received from all sites.

  Second, when a transaction releases an X mode region lock, the timestamp for the lock is set to the current value of TS_ctr at the site. When this lock is called back by the GLM, this value is also sent and is associated with the lock by the GLM. When received by another site, the timestamp is used to ensure that log records for conflicting actions covered by this lock have increasing timestamp values. As an optimization, the site identifier can also be sent with the lock to the GLM; the purpose will become clear in the next point.

- **Lock Acquisition:** When a site receives an X mode region lock from the GLM, it sets its own TS_ctr to be the maximum of its current TS_ctr and the timestamp associated with the lock (received from the GLM). Further, the lock is granted to a local transaction only after all outstanding (unapplied) updates at the time of acquiring the lock have been applied to the page. This is to ensure that data accessed at a site is always the most recent version of the data.

  As an optimization, if a site identifier is provided with the lock by the GLM, it suffices to process log records up to (and including) the log record from the site with the timestamp provided.

7.3. Checkpointing

Checkpointing is coordinated by one of the sites. The checkpointing operation consists of three steps — 1) writing the database image by the coordinator, 2) writing the ATT at each site and 3) flushing the logs at each site. The main difference from the centralized case lies in how each step is carried out. We describe each step below:

1. The coordinator announces the beginning of the checkpoint, at which time all other sites first make a copy of their dpts and then subsequently zero their dpts, and note their current end_of_stable_log values. Note that recording end_of_stable_log and dpt, and then zeroing dpt is done atomically with respect to flushes. Every site sends the recorded dpt and end_of_stable_log values to the coordinator. The coordinator site j applies all outstanding updates, then atomically (with respect to processing further log records and flushing) records its end_of_stable_log, copies its timestamp array A_j to A_C, copies its dpt to ckpt_dpt, and then zeroes its own dpt. The coordinator then or's its ckpt_dpt with the copies of the dpts it receives from the other sites. It then writes to the checkpoint image the ckpt_dpt, the end_of_stable_logs for each site, and the timestamp array A_C.

   Next, the database image is written out by the coordinator in the same fashion as in the centralized case, writing out not only pages dirty in this checkpoint interval (in ckpt_dpt), but also pages dirtied in the previous checkpoint interval (in the ckpt_dpt stored in the previous checkpoint).

2. Once the coordinator has written out the database image, it instructs each site to write out its ATT. Multiple sites can be concurrently writing out their ATTs.

3. The logs are flushed at each site and after all sites flush their logs the coordinator commits the checkpoint by toggling cur_ckpt, as in the centralized case.

Note that in Step 1, applying outstanding updates at the coordinator before recording ckpt_dpt and A_C ensures that updates preceding end_of_stable_log reported by other sites have been applied to the database pages, and thus, it is safe to zero dpts at sites when end_of_stable_log is noted. Also, since each site notes end_of_stable_log independently, it is possible that for a redo log record after end_of_stable_log at one site, a conflicting redo log record generated after it may be before end_of_stable_log noted at a different site. As a result, during restart recovery, applying every update after end_of_stable_log in the system log for a site could result in the latter update being lost. Storing A_C in the checkpoint and during restart recovery, applying only redo records at site i whose timestamps are greater than $A_C[i]$ eliminates the above problem since timestamps for both updates would be smaller than the corresponding TS_ctr values for the sites in A_C.

7.4. Recovery

Restart recovery in case of a system wide failure (where all sites have to be recovered) can be performed as follows by an arbitrary site j in the system, which we will call the acting coordinator. The following actions are performed by site j alone.

First, the database image and the checkpointed timestamp array A_C are read, and for each site, the ATT and the end_of_stable_log recorded in the checkpoint are read. Redo log records in the system logs for the various sites are then applied to the database image by concurrently scanning the various system logs. Each site's system log is scanned in parallel, starting from the end_of_stable_log recorded for the site in the checkpoint. At each point, if the next log record to be considered in any of the system logs is not a redo log record, then it is processed and the ATT for its site is modified as described for the centralized case in Section 2.7. On the other hand, if the next record to be considered in all the system logs is a redo log record, then the log record considered next is the one (among all the system logs on disk being considered) with the lowest timestamp value. For every redo log record encountered in the system log for a site, i, with a timestamp greater than $A_C[i]$, the update is applied and the affected pages are marked as dirty in j's dpt.

Once all the system logs have been scanned, TS_ctr at site j is set to the largest timestamp contained in a redo log record. In-progress operations in the ATTs for the various sites are then rolled back and executed, respectively, at site j against the database at site j, beginning with level L_0 and then considering successive levels L_1, L_2 and so on (as described in Section 2.7). When an operation in an ATT entry for a site is being processed, actions are performed on the undo and redo logs for the entry. Furthermore, when an operation pre-commits/aborts, log records from the redo log are appended to the system log for the site and the timestamp for each redo log record appended is obtained by incrementing TS_ctr at site j.

Finally, every site's system logs are flushed causing appropriate pages in j's dpt to be marked dirty (updates are not broadcast, however), and the TS_ctr at every site and $A_k[i]$ for all sites k and i are set to the TS_ctr value at site j. The database image at every site is copied from the database image at site j, the dpt for each site is copied from the dpt at site j; recovery is then complete.

7.5. Overview of Correctness

The correctness of the checkpointing and recovery algorithms follows from the following properties.

1. If the timestamp contained in a log record for site i is less than or equal to $A_C[i]$, then the log record's effects must have made it to the copy of the database in the checkpoint.

2. Any log record in the system log for site i prior to end_of_stable_log for the site has a timestamp less than or equal to $A_C[i]$.

3. If L_1 and L_2 are conflicting log records and L_1 is generated before L_2, then if L_2 is flushed to the stable log, then so is L_1.

4. If L_1 and L_2 are conflicting log records in different system logs and L_1 is generated before L_2, then L_1 has a lower timestamp than L_2.

Property (1) holds since when a page is written to disk during a checkpoint at site j, updates preceding $A_j[i]$ have made it to the image of the page at site j (due to the algorithm for application of incoming log records), and this page is dirty in j's dpt (because the dpt is noted atomically with A_C).

Property (2) holds since before site i sends its end_of_stable_log to the checkpoint coordinator, any update preceding it is sent to the coordinator (when the system log is flushed at site i). Since the network is FIFO, the receipt of the end_of_stable_log implies that all necessary log records have arrived. Furthermore, before noting $A_C[i]$, the coordinator applies outstanding updates from site i and thus sets $A_j[i]$ to the timestamp of the last update applied from site i.

Property (3) holds since the log is flushed every time a site relinquishes a region lock. Finally, property (4) holds since before the region lock that guards L_1 is released by its site, L_1 is appended to the system log and assigned a timestamp from the TS_ctr at the site. Furthermore, the TS_ctr at L_1's site is shipped along with the region lock when it releases the region lock, and the site for L_2 sets its TS_ctr to be at least the timestamp it receives when it acquires the lock. Thus, since L_2 is generated after the lock is obtained by its site, it is assigned a timestamp greater than the TS_ctr value at its site when the site receives the region lock, and the property holds.

From the above properties, it follows that history is repeated as a consequence of applying the redo log records contained in the system logs in timestamp order during restart recovery. From properties (1) and (2), it follows that log records preceding end_of_stable_log can be ignored since these updates are already contained in the checkpoint image. Similarly, property (2) implies that updates at a site i by a log record do not need to be applied if $A_C[i]$ is greater than or equal to the timestamp in the log record. Property (3) ensures that log records in the system logs accurately and completely describe the history of updates to every region. Finally, property (4) ensures that conflicting updates described by log records that appear after end_of_stable_log are applied during recovery in the order in which they were performed during normal processing. Note that, for conflicting log records L_1 and L_2, L_1 generated before L_2, L_2 may precede end_of_stable_log for its site (say i), while L_1 follows end_of_stable_log for its site. In this case, due to property (2), $A_C[i]$ would be greater than or equal to the timestamp for L_2 and the timestamp for L_2 would be greater than that for L_1. Thus, the update by L_1 would not be applied during recovery.

7.6. Recovery from Site Failure

Our recovery algorithm can also be extended to deal with a site failure *without* performing a complete system restart, so long as the GLM data has not been lost, or can be regenerated from the other sites. If this is not the case, a full system recovery is performed instead. Recovery from site failure, as with regular system recovery, has a redo pass, followed by rollback of in-progress operations.

Before beginning the redo recovery pass, the recovering site, say j, retrieves from the most recent checkpoint the database image, the ATT for site j, the timestamp array A_C and the end_of_stable_log for each site. It then informs other sites that it is up, and requests from each site i, that site's current end_of_stable_log value, and the value of $A_i[j]$. At this point, other sites start sending log records to j; these are buffered and processed later. The redo pass is then performed by scanning all the system logs as described in the previous subsection except that 1) only the pages in the dpt for site j are marked dirty, 2) only actions on the ATT for site j are performed, and 3) the system log for a site is scanned until the end_of_stable_log returned by that site at the beginning of site j's recovery.

Also, log records in the tail end of the log of the recovering site may not have made it to other sites – since a log record is broadcast after it is flushed. For each site i (other than the recovering site, j) all log records in site j's system log that have timestamps greater than $A_i[j]$ are broadcast to site i as they are processed. Once the redo pass is completed, $A_j[i]$ is set to the maximum timestamp in a redo log record encountered during the redo pass in the system log for site i. Also, TS_ctr at site j is set to the maximum of $A_j[i]$ for all sites i. At this point, site j can begin applying updates described by log records received from other sites, as during normal processing, in the order received, and checkpoints can again be taken as normal.

Before rolling back in-progress operations, the locks that were cached at site j at the time it crashed are re-obtained by the recovery process at site j by consulting the GLM. As described in Section 2.7, rollback is performed level by level, with additional locks requested as is done during normal processing (see Section 7.2). Thus, TS_ctr at site j is incremented and outstanding updates are applied when a new lock is obtained, TS_ctr is incremented when a redo log record is appended to the system log, and log flushes are performed when operation/X mode region locks are released by site j. Also, level L_i operation locks at site j can be released once all active operations at level L_{i+1} have been rolled back.

8. Conclusion

In this paper, we showed how our single-site multi-level recovery algorithm for main-memory databases can be extended to a distributed-memory data-shipping system while maintaining many of the original benefits of the single-site algorithm. The first scheme presented supports client-server processing in which a central system controls logs and checkpoints. In the second and third scheme, suitable for a cluster of computers with a shared disk, sites participate symmetrically in transaction processing activities.

We described details of recovery after the failure of clients or the server in the client-server case, and from single site as well as system-wide failure in the shared disk case. Our schemes allow concurrent updates at multiple clients in a client-server environment or multiple sites of the shared disk environment. By allowing fine-grained and flexible concurrency control, our schemes are applicable to a range of distributed, main-memory applications which need transactional access to data.

Our distributed schemes are based on a multi-level scheme for recovery in main-memory databases which has been implemented in the Dalí Main Memory Storage Manager [9]. Thus, the benefits of this algorithm are extended to the distributed schemes; the benefits include fuzzy checkpointing, use of the log for implementing functions that otherwise require page latching, low overhead logging with undo records written only due to a checkpoint, and per-transaction logs for low contention.

Future work includes parallelization of recovery in the shared disk setting, and recovery in a system where not all sites store the entire database. We also plan to explore the performance of our schemes through experimentation, and then build a distributed, data-shipping version of Dali based on these algorithms.

Notes

1. It is possible to release locks for a transaction on pre-commit; as a result read-only transactions may read uncommitted data, and their commit must be delayed until the dirty data they have read has been committed.
2. The logs can be deleted on pre-commit, since, short of a system crash, nothing can result in the transaction aborting.
3. In cases when region sizes change, certain additional region locks on storage allocation structures may need to be obtained. For example, in a page based system, if an update causes the size of a tuple to change, then in addition to a region lock on the tuple, an X mode region lock on the storage allocation structures on the page must be obtained.

References

1. P. Bohannon, D. Lieuwen, R. Rastogi, S. Seshadri, S. Sudarshan, and A. Silberschatz. The architecture of the Dali main-memory storage manager. *Multimedia Tools and Applications*, 4(2):115–151, March 1997.
2. P. Bohannon, J. Parker, R. Rastogi, S. Seshadri, and S. Sudarshan. Distributed multi-level recovery in main-memory databases. Technical Report 112530-96-02-27-01TM, Lucent Technologies, Bell Laboratories, February 1996.
3. M. J. Carey, D. J. DeWitt, M. J. Franklin, N. E. Hall, M. L. McAuliffe, J. F. Naughton, D. T. Schuh, M. H. Solomon, C. K. Tan, O. G. Tsatalos, S. J. White, and M. J. Zwilling. Shoring up persistent applications. In *Proceedings of ACM-SIGMOD 1994 International Conference on Management of Data, Minneapolis, Minnesota*, pages 383–394, May 1994.
4. M. J. Carey, M. J. Franklin, and M. Zaharioudakis. Fine-grained sharing in a page server OODBMS. In *Proceedings of ACM-SIGMOD 1994 International Conference on Management of Data, Minneapolis, Minnesota*, pages 359–370, May 1994.
5. D. J. DeWitt, R. Katz, F. Olken, D. Shapiro, M. Stonebraker, and D. Wood. Implementation techniques for main memory database systems. *Proc. ACM-SIGMOD 1984 Int'l Conf. on Management of Data*, pages 1–8, June 1984.
6. M. J. Franklin, M. J. Zwilling, C. K. Tan, M. J. Carey, and D. J. DeWitt. Crash recovery in client-server EXODUS. In *Proceedings of ACM-SIGMOD 1992 International Conference on Management of Data, San Diego, California*, pages 165–174, June 1992.
7. H. Garcia-Molina and K. Salem. Main memory database systems: An overview. *IEEE Transactions on Knowledge and Data Engineering*, 4(6):509–516, December 1992.
8. Robert B. Hagmann. A crash recovery scheme for a memory-resident database system. *IEEE Transactions on Computers*, C-35(9):839–847, September 1986.
9. H.V. Jagadish, Dan Lieuwen, Rajeev Rastogi, Avi Silberschatz, and S. Sudarshan. Dali: A high performance main-memory storage manager. In *Procs. of the International Conf. on Very Large Databases*, 1994.
10. H.V. Jagadish, Avi Silberschatz, and S. Sudarshan. Recovering from main-memory lapses. In *Procs. of the International Conf. on Very Large Databases*, 1993.
11. C. Lamb, G. Landis, J. Orenstein, and D. Weinreb. The objectstore database system. *Communications of the ACM*, 34(10), October 1991.
12. T. Lehman, E. J. Shekita, and L. Cabrera. An evaluation of Starburst's memory resident storage component. *IEEE Transactions on Knowledge and Data Engineering*, 4(6):555–566, December 1992.
13. D. Lomet. MLR: A recovery method for multi-level systems. In *Proceedings of ACM-SIGMOD 1992 International Conference on Management of Data, San Diego, California*, pages 185–194, 1992.

14. C. Mohan, D. Haderle, B. Lindsay, H. Pirahesh, and P. Schwarz. ARIES: A transaction recovery method supporting fine-granularity locking and partial rollbacks using write-ahead logging. *ACM Transactions on Database Systems*, 17(1):94–162, March 1992.

15. C. Mohan and I. Narang. Recovery and coherency-control protocols for fast intersystem page transfer and fine-granularity locking in a shared disks transaction environment. In *Proceedings of the Seventeenth International Conference on Very Large Databases, Barcelona*, pages 193–207, September 1991.

16. C. Mohan and I. Narang. ARIES/CSA: a method for database recovery in client-server architectures. In *Proceedings of ACM-SIGMOD 1994 International Conference on Management of Data, Minneapolis, Minnesota*, pages 55–66, May 1994.

17. E. Rahm. Recovery concepts for data sharing systems. In *Proceedings of the Twenty first International Conference on Fault-Tolerant Computing (FTCS-21), Montreal*, pages 109–123, June 1991.

18. K. Salem and H. Garcia-Molina. System M: A transaction processing testbed for memory resident data. *IEEE Transactions on Knowledge and Data Engineering*, 2(1):161–172, March 1990.

19. K. Salem and H. Garcia-Molina. System M: A transaction processing testbed for memory resident data. *IEEE Transactions on Knowledge and Data Engineering*, 2(1):161–172, 1990.

20. G. Weikum, C. Hasse, P. Broessler, and P. Muth. Multi-level recovery. In *Proceedings of the Nineth ACM SIGACT-SIGMOD-SIGART Symposium on Principles of Database Systems, Nashville*, pages 109–123, June 1990.

Distributed and Parallel Databases, 6, 73–110 (1998)
© 1998 Kluwer Academic Publishers.

Capabilities-Based Query Rewriting in Mediator Systems * **

YANNIS PAPAKONSTANTINOU   yannis@cs.ucsd.edu
UCSD, Computer Science & Engineering, La Jolla, CA 92093-0114

ASHISH GUPTA   ashish@junglee.com
Junglee Corp., 4149B El Camino Way, Palo Alto, CA 94306

LAURA HAAS   laura@almaden.ibm.com
IBM Almaden Research Center, 650 Harry Road, San Jose, CA 95120

Recommended by: Jeffrey F. Naughton and Gerhard Weikum

Abstract. Users today are struggling to integrate a broad range of information sources providing different levels of query capabilities. Currently, data sources with different and limited capabilities are accessed either by writing rich functional wrappers for the more primitive sources, or by dealing with all sources at a "lowest common denominator". This paper explores a third approach, in which a mediator ensures that sources receive queries they can handle, while still taking advantage of all of the query power of the source. We propose an architecture that enables this, and identify a key component of that architecture, the *Capabilities-Based Rewriter (CBR)*. The CBR takes as input a description of the capabilities of a data source, and a query targeted for that data source. From these, the CBR determines component queries to be sent to the sources, commensurate with their abilities, and computes a plan for combining their results using joins, unions, selections, and projections. We provide a language to describe the query capability of data sources and a plan generation algorithm. Our description language and plan generation algorithm are schema independent and handle SPJ queries. We also extend CBR with a cost-based optimizer. The net effect is that we prune without losing completeness. Finally we compare the implementation of a CBR for the Garlic project with the algorithms proposed in this paper.

Keywords: heterogeneous sources, mediator systems, query rewriting, query containment, cost optimization

1. Introduction

Organizations today must integrate multiple heterogeneous information sources, many of which are not conventional SQL database management systems. Examples of such information sources include bibliographic databases, object repositories, chemical structure databases, WAIS servers, etc. Some of these systems provide powerful query capabilities, while others are much more limited. A new challenge for the database community is to allow users to query this data using a single powerful query language, with location transparency, despite the diverse capabilities of the underlying systems.

Figure (1.a) shows one commonly proposed integration architecture [2, 16, 4, 1]. Each data source has a *wrapper*, which provides a view of the data in that source in a common

---
* Research partially supported by Wright Laboratories, Wright Patterson AFB, ARPA Contract F33615-93-C-1337.
** This paper is an extended version of a paper published in International Conference on Parallel and Distributed Information Systems, December 1996.

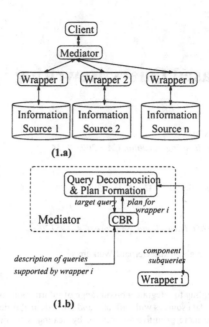

Figure 1. (a) A typical integration architecture. (b) CBR-mediator interaction.

data model. Each wrapper can translate queries expressed in the common language to the language of its underlying information source. The *mediator* provides an integrated view of the data exported by the wrappers. In particular, when the mediator receives a query from a client, it determines what data it needs from each underlying wrapper, sends the wrappers individual queries to collect the required data, and combines the responses to produce the query result.

This scenario works well when all wrappers can support any query over their data. However, in the types of systems we consider, this assumption is unrealistic. It leads to extremely complex wrappers, needed to support a powerful query interface against possibly quite limited data sources. For example, in many systems the relational data model is taken as the common data model, and all wrappers must provide a full SQL interface, even if the underlying data source is a file system, or a hierarchical DBMS. Alternatively, this assumption may lead to a "lowest common denominator" approach in which only simple queries are sent to the wrappers. In this case, the search capabilities of more sophisticated data sources are not exploited, and hence the mediator is forced to do most of the work, resulting in unnecessarily poor performance. We would like to have simple wrappers that accurately reflect the search capabilities of the underlying data source. To enable this, the mediator must recognize differences and limitations in capabilities, and ensure that wrappers receive only queries that they can handle.

For Garlic [2], an integrator of heterogeneous multimedia data being developed at IBM's Almaden Research Center, such an understanding is essential. Garlic needs to deal efficiently with the disparate data types and querying capabilities needed by applications as diverse as medical, advertising, pharmaceutical research, and computer-aided design. In our model, a wrapper is capable of handling some set of queries, known as the *supported queries* for that wrapper. When the mediator receives a query from a client, it decomposes it into a set of queries, each of which references data at a single wrapper. We call these individual queries *target queries* for the wrappers. A target query need not be a supported query; it may sometimes be necessary to further decompose it into simpler supported *Component SubQueries (CSQs)* in order to execute it. A *plan* combines the results of the CSQs to produce the answer to the target query.

To obtain this functionality, we explored a *Capabilities-Based Rewriter (CBR)* module (Figure 1.b) as part of the Garlic query engine (mediator). The CBR uses a description of each wrapper's ability, expressed in a special purpose *query capabilities description language*, to develop a plan for the wrapper's target query.

The mediator decomposes a user's query into target queries q for each wrapper w without considering whether q is supported by w. It then passes q to the CBR for "inspection." The CBR compares q against the description of the queries supported by wrapper w, and produces a plan p for q, if either (i) q is directly supported by w, or (ii) q is computable by the mediator through a plan that involves selection, projection and join of CSQs that are supported by w. The mediator then combines the individual plans p into a complete plan for the user's query.

The CBR allows a clean separation of wrapper capabilities from mediator internals. Wrappers are "thin" modules that translate queries in the common model into source-specific queries.[1] Hence, wrappers reflect the actual capabilities of the underlying data sources, while the mediator has a general mechanism for interpreting those capabilities and forming execution strategies for queries. This paper focuses on the technology needed to enable the CBR approach. We first present a language for describing wrappers' query capabilities. The descriptions look like context-free grammars, modified to describe queries rather than arbitrary strings. The descriptions may be recursive, thus allowing the description of infinitely large supported queries. In addition, they may be schema-independent. For example, we may describe the capabilities of a relational database wrapper without referring to the schema of a specific relational database. An additional benefit of the grammar-like description language is that it can be appropriately augmented with actions to translate a target query to a query of the underlying information system. This feature has been described in [14] and we will not discuss it further in this paper.

The second contribution of this paper is an architecture for the CBR and an algorithm to build plans for a target query using the CSQs supported by the relevant wrapper. This problem is a generalization of the problem of determining if a query can be answered using a set of materialized queries/views [9, 18]. However, the CBR uses a description of potentially infinite queries as opposed to a finite set of materialized views. The problem of identifying CSQs that compute the target query has many sources of exponentiality even for the restricted case discussed by [9, 18]. The CBR algorithm uses optimizations and heuristics to eliminate sources of exponentiality in many common cases.

The third contribution of this paper, which does not appear in [15], is the incorporation of cost-based optimization into the CBR. The described cost-based prunings do *not* compromise the completeness of the algorithm, i.e., if there is a supported plan the algorithm will find it.

Finally, we compare the algorithms of this paper with the algorithms that were eventually implemented for the Garlic system. The implementation uses the extensible optimizer of Starburst, hence having an excellent framework for combining capabilities-based rewriting with cost-based optimization. On the other hand, the use of Starburst's optimizer required changes in the description language and corresponding changes in the algorithms.

In the next section, we present the language used to describe a wrapper's query capabilities. In Section 3 we describe the basic architecture of the CBR, identifying three modules: Component SubQuery Discovery, Plan Construction, and Plan Refinement. These components are detailed in Sections 4, 5 and 6, respectively. Section 7 discusses the combination of CBR with cost-based optimization. Section 8 compares the proposed CBR algorithms against the CBR implementation of Garlic. Section 9 summarizes the run-time performance of the CBR. Section 10 discusses related work. Finally, Section 11 concludes with some directions for future work in this area.

2. The Relational Query Description Language(RQDL)

RQDL is the language we use to describe a wrapper's supported queries. We discuss only Select-Project-Join queries in this paper. In section 2.1 we introduce the basic language features , followed in sections 2.2 and 2.3 by the extensions needed to describe infinite query sets and to support schema-independent descriptions. Section 2.4 introduces a normal form for queries and descriptors that increases the precision of the language. The complete language specification appears in Appendix A.1.

The description language focuses on conjunctive queries. We have found that it is powerful enough to express the abilities of many wrappers and sources, such as lookup catalogs and object databases. Indeed, it is more expressive than context-free grammars.[2]

2.1. Language Basics

An RQDL specification contains a set of *query templates*, each of which is essentially a parameterized query. Where an actual query might have a constant, the query template has a *constant placeholder*, allowing it to represent many queries of the same form. In addition, we allow the values assumed by the constant placeholders to be restricted by specifier-provided *metapredicates*. A query is described by a template (loosely speaking) if (1) each predicate in the query matches one predicate in the template, and vice versa, and (2) any metapredicates on the placeholders of the template evaluate to true for the matching constants in the query. The order of the predicates in query and template need not be the same, and different variable names are of course possible.

For example, consider a "lookup" facility that provides information – such as name, department, office address, and so on – about the employees of a company. The "lookup" facility can either retrieve all employees, or retrieve employees whose last name has a specific prefix, or retrieve employees whose last name and first name have specific prefixes.[3] We integrate "lookup" into our heterogeneous system by creating a wrapper, called lookup, that exports a predicate emp(First-Name, Last-Name, Department, Office, Manager). (The Manager field may be 'Y' or 'N'.) The wrapper also exports a predicate prefix(Full, Prefix) that is successful when its second argument is a prefix of its first argument. This second argument must be a string, consisting of letters only. We may write the following Datalog query to retrieve emp tuples for persons whose first name starts with 'Rak' and whose last name starts with 'Aggr':

(Q1) answer(FN,LN,D,O,M) :- emp(FN,LN,D,O,M),
         prefix(FN,'Rak'), prefix(LN,'Aggr')

In this paper we use Datalog [23] as our query language because it is well-suited to handling SPJ queries and facilitates the discussion of our algorithms.[4] We use the following Datalog terms in this paper: *Distinguished variables* are the variables that appear in the target query head. A *join variable* is any variable that appears twice or more in the target query tail. In the query (Q1) the distinguished variables are FN, LN, D, O and M and the join variables are FN and LN.

Description (D2) is an RQDL specification of lookup's query capabilities. The identifiers starting with $ ($FP and $LP) are constant placeholders. _isalpha() is a metapredicate that returns true if its argument is a string that contains letters only. Metapredicates start with an underscore and a lowercase letter. Intuitively, template (QT2.3) describes query (Q1) because the predicates of the query match those of the template (despite differences in order and in variable names), and the metapredicates evaluate to true when $FP is mapped to 'Rak' and $LP to 'Aggr'.

(D2) answer(F,L,D,O,M) :-   (QT2.1)
         emp(F,L,D,O,M)
     answer(F,L,D,O,M) :-   (QT2.2)
         emp(F,L,D,O,M),
         prefix(L, $LP), _isalpha($LP)
     answer(F,L,D,O,M) :-   (QT2.3)
         emp(F,L,D,O,M),
         prefix(L, $LP), prefix(F,$FP),
         _isalpha($LP), _isalpha($FP)

In general, a template describes any query that can be produced by the following steps:

1. *Map* each placeholder to a constant, e.g., map $LP to 'Aggr'.
2. *Map* each template variable to a query variable, e.g., map F to FN.
3. *Evaluate* the metapredicates and discard any template that contains at least one metapredicate that evaluates to false.
4. *Permute* the template's subgoals.

2.2. Descriptions of Large and Infinite Sets of Supported Queries

RQDL can describe arbitrarily large sets of templates (and hence queries) when extended with nonterminals as in context-free grammars. Nonterminals are represented by identifiers that start with an underscore (_) and a capital letter. They have zero or more parameters and they are associated with *nonterminal templates*. A query template t containing nonterminals describes a query q if there is an *expansion* of t that describes q. An expansion of t is obtained by replacing each nonterminal N of t with one of the nonterminal templates that define N until there is no nonterminal in t.

For example, assume that lookup allows us to pose one or more substring conditions on one or more fields of emp. For example, we may pose query (Q3), which retrieves the data for employees whose office contains the strings 'alma' and 'B'.

```
(Q3) answer(F,L,D,O,M) :- emp(F,L,D,O,M),
      substring(O,'alma'), substring(O,'B')
```

(D4) uses the nonterminal _Cond to describe the supported queries. In this description the query template (QT4.1) is supported by nonterminal templates such as (NT4.1).

```
(D4)answer(F,L,D,O,M) :-                                          (QT4.1)
    emp(F,L,D,O,M), _Cond(F,L,D,O,M)
_Cond(F,L,D,O,M) :                                                (NT4.1)
    substring(F, $FS), _Cond(F,L,D,O,M)
_Cond(F,L,D,O,M) :                                                (NT4.2)
    substring(L, $LS), _Cond(F,L,D,O,M)
_Cond(F,L,D,O,M) :                                                (NT4.3)
    substring(D, $DS), _Cond(F,L,D,O,M)
_Cond(F,L,D,O,M) :                                                (NT4.4)
    substring(O,$OS), _Cond(F,L,D,O,M)
_Cond(F,L,D,O,M) :                                                (NT4.5)
    substring(M, $MS), _Cond(F,L,D,O,M)
_Cond(F,L,D,O,M) :                                                (NT4.6)
```

To see that description (D4) describes query (Q3), we expand _Cond(F,L,D,O,M) in (QT4.1) with the nonterminal template (NT4.4) and then again expand _Cond with the same template. The _Cond subgoal in the resulting expansion is expanded by the empty template (NT4.6) to obtain expansion (E5).

```
(E5) answer(F,L,D,O,M) :- emp(F,L,D,O,M),
      substring(O,$OS), substring(O,$OS1)
```

Before a template is used for expansion, all of its variables are renamed to be unique. Hence, the second occurrence of placeholder $OS of template (NT4.4) is renamed to $OS1 in (E5). (E5) describes query (Q3), *i.e.*, the placeholders and variables of (E5) can be mapped to the constants and variables of (Q3).

2.3. Schema Independent Descriptions of Supported Queries

Description (D4) assumes that the wrapper exports a fixed schema. However, the query capabilities of many sources (and thus wrappers) are independent of the schemas of the data that reside in them. For example, a relational database allows SPJ queries on all of its relations. To support schema independent descriptions RQDL allows the use of placeholders in place of the relation name. Furthermore, to allow tables of arbitrary arity and column names, RQDL provides special variables called *vector variables*, or simply vectors, that match lists of variables that appear in a query. We represent vectors in our examples by identifiers starting with an underscore (_). In addition, we provide two built-in metapredicates to relate vectors and attributes: **_subset** and **_in**. **_subset**(_R, _A) succeeds if each variable in the list that matches _R appears in the list that matches _A. **_in**($Position, X, _A) succeeds if _A matches a variable list, and there is a query variable that matches X and appears at the position number that matches $Position. (For readability we will use *italics* for vectors and **bold** for metapredicates).

For example, consider a wrapper called file-wrap that accesses tables residing in plain UNIX files. It may output any subset of any table's fields and may impose one or more substring conditions on any field. Such a wrapper may be easily implemented using the UNIX utility AWK. (D6) uses vectors and the built-in metapredicates to describe the queries supported by file-wrap.

```
(D6) (QT6.1) answer(_R)  :- $Table(_A),
                _Cond(_A), _subset(_R, _A)
     (NT6.1) _Cond(_A) :_in($Position,X,_A),
                substring(X,$S), _Cond(_A)
     (NT6.2) _Cond(_A) :
```

In general, to decide whether a query is described by a template containing vectors we must expand the nonterminals, map the variables, placeholders, and vectors, and finally, evaluate any metapredicates. To illustrate this, we show how to verify that query (Q7) is described by (D6).

```
(Q7) answer(L,D)  :- emp(F,L,D,O,M),
     substring(O,'alma'), substring(O,'B')
```

First, we expand (QT6.1) by replacing the nonterminal _Cond with (NT6.1) twice, and then with (NT6.2), thus obtaining expansion (E8).

```
(E8) answer(_R)  :- $Table(_A),
     _in($Position,X,_A),substring(X,$S),
     _in($Position1,X1,_A),substring(X1,$S1),
     _subset(_R,_A)
```

Expansion (E8) describes query (Q7) because there is a mapping of variables, vectors, and placeholders of (E8) that makes the metapredicates succeed and makes every predicate of the expansion identical to a predicate of the query. Namely, vector _A is mapped to [F,L,D,O,M], vector _R to [L,D], placeholders $Position and $Position1 to 4, $S to 'alma', $S1 to 'B', and the variables X and X1 to O. We must be careful with vector mappings; if the vector _V that maps to $[X_1, \ldots, X_n]$ appears in a metapredicate, we replace _V with $[X_1, \ldots, X_n]$. However, if the vector _V appears in a predicate as $p(\_V)$ the mapping results in $p(X_1, \ldots, X_n)$. Finally, the metapredicate **_in**(4, O, [F,L,D,O,M])

succeeds because 0 is the fourth variable of the list, and _subset([L,D], [F,L,D,O,M])
succeeds because [L,D] is a "subset" of [F,L,D,O,M].

Vectors are useful even when the schema is known as the specification may otherwise
be repetitious, as in description (D4). In our running example, even though we know the
attributes of emp, we save effort by not having to explicitly mention all of the column names
to say that a substring condition can be placed on any column.

2.4. Query and Description Normal Form

If we allow templates' variables and vectors to map to arbitrary lists of constants and
variables, descriptions may appear to support queries that the underlying wrapper does not
support. This is because using the same variable name in different places in the query
or description can cause an implicit join or selection that does not explicitly appear in
the description. For example, consider query (Q9), which retrieves employees where the
manager field is 'Y' and the first and last names are equal, as denoted by the double
appearance of FL in emp.

(Q9) answer(FL,D) :- emp(FL,FL,D,O,'Y')

(D6) should not describe query (Q9). Nevertheless, we can construct expansion (E10),
which erroneously matches query (Q9) if we map _A to [FL,FL,D,O,'Y'] and _R to
[FL,D]:

(E10) answer(_R):-$Table(_A), _subset(_R,_A)

This section introduces a query and description *normal form* that avoids inadvertently
describing joins and selections that were not intended. In the normal form both queries and
descriptions have only explicit equalities. A query is normalized by replacing every constant
c with a unique variable V and then by introducing the subgoal $V = c$. Furthermore, for
every join variable V that appears $n > 1$ times in the query we replace its instances with
the unique variables $V_1, \ldots, V_n$ and introduce the subgoals $V_i = V_j, i = 1, \ldots, n, j =
1 \ldots, i - 1$. We replace any appearance of V in the head with V_1. For example, query
(Q11) is the normal form of (Q9).

(Q11) answer(FL1,D) :- employee(FL1,FL2,D,O,M),
      FL1=FL2, M='Y'

Description (D6) does not describe (Q11) because (D6) does not support the equality conditions that appear in (Q11). Description (D12) supports equality conditions on any column
and equalities between any two columns: (NT12.2) describes equalities with constants and
(NT12.3) describes equalities between the columns of our table.

(D12) answer(_R) :-   (QT12.1)
      $Table(_A), _Cond(_A), _subset(_R, _A)
      _Cond(_A) :   (NT12.1)
      _in($Position,X,_A), substring(X, $S),
      _Cond(_A)

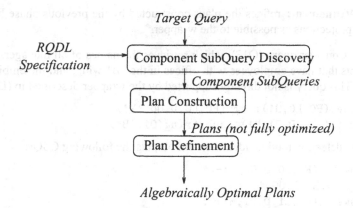

Figure 2. The CBR's components

_Cond(_A) :   (NT12.2)
  _in($Position1,X,_A), X=$C, _Cond(_A)
_Cond(_A) :   (NT12.3)
  _in($Pos1,X,_A), _in($Pos2,Y,_A),
  X=Y, _Cond(_A)
_Cond(_A) :   (NT12.4)

For presentation purposes we use the more compact unnormalized form of queries and descriptions when there is no danger of introducing inadvertent selections and joins. However, the algorithms rely on the normal form.

3. The Capabilities-Based Rewriter

The Capabilities-Based Rewriter (CBR) determines whether a target query q is directly supported by the appropriate wrapper, *i.e.*, whether it matches the description d of the wrapper's capabilities. If not, the CBR determines whether q can be computed by combining a set of supported queries (using selections, projections and joins). In this case, the CBR will produce a set of plans for evaluating the query. The CBR consists of three modules, which are invoked serially (see Figure 2):

- **Component SubQuery (CSQ) Discovery:** finds supported queries that involve one or more subgoals of q. The CSQs that are returned contain the largest possible number of selections and joins, and do no projection. All other CSQs are pruned. This prevents an exponential explosion in the number of CSQs.

- **Plan Construction:** produces one or more plans that compute q by combining the CSQs exported by CSQ Discovery. The plan construction algorithm is based on query subsumption and has been tuned to perform efficiently in the cases typically arising in capabilities-based rewriting.

- **Plan Refinement:** refines the plans constructed by the previous phase by pushing as many projections as possible to the wrapper.

Example: Consider query (Q13), which retrieves the names of all managers that manage departments that have employees with offices in the 'B' wing, and the employees' office numbers. This query is not directly supported by the wrapper described in (D12).

```
(Q13) answer(FO,LO,O1):-emp(FO,LO,D,OO,'Y'),
        emp(F1,L1,D,O1,M1), substring(O1,'B')
```

The CSQ detection module identifies and outputs the following CSQs:

```
(Q14) answer₁₄(FO,LO,D,OO) :-
        emp(FO,LO,D,OO,'Y')
(Q15) answer₁₅(F1,L1,D,O1,M1) :-
        emp(F1,L1,D,O1,M1), substring(O1, 'B')
```

Note, the CSQ discovery module does not output the 2^4 CSQs that have the tail of (Q14) but export a different subset of the variables FO, LO, D, and OO (likewise for (Q15). The CSQs that export fewer variables are pruned.

The plan construction module detects that a join on D of answer₁₄ and answer₁₅ produces the required answer of (Q13). Consequently, it derives the plan (P16).

```
 (P16) answer(FO,LO,O1) :-
          answer₁₄(FO,LO,D,OO),
          answer₁₅(F1,L1,D,O1,M1)
```

Finally, the plan refinement module detects that variables OO, F1, L1, and M1 in answer₁₄ and answer₁₅ are unnecessary. Consequently, it generates the more efficient plan (P19).

```
(Q17) answer₁₇(FO,LO,D) :-
        emp(FO,LO,D,OO,'Y')
(Q18) answer₁₈(D,O1) :-
        emp(F1,L1,D,O1,M1), substring(O1, 'B')
(P19) answer(FO,LO,O1) :-
        answer₁₇(FO,LO,D),  answer₁₈(D,O1)
```

□

The CBR's goal is to produce all *algebraically optimal* plans for evaluating the query. An algebraically optimal plan is one in which any selection, projection or join that can be done in the wrapper is done there, and in which there are no unnecessary queries. More formally:

Definition. Algebraically Optimal Plan P A plan P is algebraically optimal if there is no other plan P' such that for every CSQ s of P there is a corresponding CSQ s' of P' such that the set of subgoals of s' is a superset of the set of subgoals of s (*i.e.*, s' has more selections and joins than s) and the set of exported variables of s is a superset of the set of exported variables of s' (*i.e.*, s' has more projections than s.)

In the next three sections we describe each of the modules of the CBR in turn.

4. CSQ Discovery

The CSQ discovery module takes as input a target query and a description. It operates as a rule production system where the templates of the description are the production rules and the subgoals of the target query are the base facts. The CSQ discovery module uses bottom-up evaluation because it is guaranteed to terminate even for recursive descriptions [24]. However, bottom-up derivation often derives unnecessary facts, unlike top-down. We use a variant of *magic sets rewriting* [24] to "focus" the bottom-up derivation. To further reduce the set of derived CSQs we develop two CSQ pruning techniques as described in Sections 4.2 and 4.3. Reducing the number of derived CSQs makes the CSQ discovery more efficient and also reduces the size of the input to the plan construction module.

The query templates derive answer facts that correspond to CSQs. In particular, a derived answer fact is the head of a produced CSQ whereas the *underlying* base facts, *i.e.*, the facts that were used for deriving answer, are the subgoals of the CSQ. Nonterminal templates derive intermediate facts that may be used by other query or nonterminal templates. We keep track of the sets of facts underlying derived facts for pruning CSQs. The following example illustrates the bottom-up derivation of CSQs and the gains that we realize from the use of the magic-sets rewriting. The next subsection discusses issues pertaining to the derivation of facts containing vectors.

Example: Consider query (Q3) and description (D4) from page 78. The subgoals emp(F,L, D,O,M), substring(O, 'alma'), and substring(O,'B') are treated by the CSQ discovery module as base facts. To distinguish the variables in target query subgoals from the templates' variables we "freeze" the variables, e.g. F,L,D,O, into similarly named constants, e.g. f,l,d,o. Actual constants like 'B' are in single quotes.

In the first round of derivations template (NT4.6) derives fact _Cond(F,L,D,U,M) without using any base fact (since the template has an empty body). Hence, the set of facts underlying the derived fact is empty. Variables are allowed in derived facts for nonterminals. The semantics is that the derived fact holds for any assignment of frozen constants to variables of the derived fact.

In the second round many templates can fire. For example, (NT4.4) derives the fact _Cond(F,L,D,o,M) using _Cond(F,L,D,O,M) and substring(o,'alma'), or using _Cond(F,L,D,o,M) and substring(o,'B'). Thus, we generate two facts that, though identical, they have different underlying sets and hence we must retain both since they may generate different CSQs. In the second round we may also fire (NT4.6) again and produce _Cond(F,L,D,O,M) but we do not retain it since its set of underlying facts is equal to the version of _Cond(F,L,D,O,M) that we have already produced.

Eventually, we generate answer(f,l,d,o,m) with set of underlying facts {emp(f,l,d,o,m), substring(o, 'alma'), substring(o,'B')}. Hence we output the CSQ (Q3), which, incidentally, is the target query.

The above process can produce an exponential number of facts. For example, we could have proved _Cond(o,L,D,O,M), _Cond(F,o,D,O,M), _Cond(o,o,D,O,M), and so on. In general, assuming that emp has n columns and we apply m substrings on it we may derive n^m facts. Magic-sets can remove this source of exponentiality by "focusing" the nonterminals. Applying magic-sets rewriting and the simplifications described in Chapter

13.4 of [24] we obtain the following equivalent description. We show only the rewriting of templates (NT4.4) and (NT4.6). The others are rewritten similarly.

```
(D20) answer(F,L,D,O,M) :-                                              (QT20.1)
        emp(F,L,D,O,M), _Cond(F,L,D,O,M)
      _Cond(F,L,D,Office,M) :                                           (NT20.4)
        mg_Cond(F,L,D,Office,M),
        substring(Office, $OS),
        _Cond(F,L,D,Office,M)
      _Cond(F,L,D,O,M) :                                                (NT20.6)
        mg_Cond(F,L,D,O,M)
      mg_Cond(F,L,D,O,M) :                                              (MS20.1)
        emp(F,L,D,O,M)
```

Now, only _Cond(f,l,d,o,m) facts (with different underlying sets) are produced. Note, the magic-sets rewritten program uses the available information in a way similar to a top-down strategy and thus derives only relevant facts. □

4.1. Derivations Involving Vectors

When the head of a nonterminal template contains a vector variable it may be possible that a derivation using this nonterminal may not be able either to bind the vector to a specific list of frozen variables or to allow the variable as is in the derived fact. The CSQ discovery module can not handle this situation. For most descriptions, magic-sets rewriting solves the problem. We demonstrate how and we formally define the set of non-problematic descriptions.

For example, let us fire template (NT6.1) of (D6) on the base facts produced by query (Q3). Assume also that (NT6.2) already derived _Cond(_A). Then we derive that _Cond(_A) holds, with set of underlying facts {substring(o, 'alma')}, provided that the constraint "_A contains o" holds. The constraint should follow the fact until _A binds to some list of frozen variables. We avoid the mess of constraints using the following magic-sets rewriting of (D6).

```
(D21) answer(_R) :-                                                     (QT21.1)
        $Table(_A), _Cond(_A),
        _subset(_R, _A)
      _Cond(_A) :                                                       (NT21.1)
        mg_Cond(_A), _in($Position,X,_A),
        substring(X,$S), _Cond(_A)
      _Cond(_A) :  mg_Cond(_A)                                          (NT21.2)
      mg_Cond(_A) :  $Table(_A)                                         (MS21.1)
```

When rules (NT21.1) and (NT21.2) fire the first subgoal instantiates variable _A to [f,l,d,o,m] and they derive only _Cond([f,l,d,o,m]). Thus, magic-sets caused _A to be bound to the only vector of interest, namely [f,l,d,o,m]. Note a program that derives facts with unbound vectors may not be problematic because no metapredicate may use the unbound vector variable. However we take a conservative approach and consider only those programs that produce facts with only bound vector variables. Magic-sets rewriting does not always ensure that derived facts have bound vectors. In the rest of this section we describe sufficient conditions for guaranteeing the derivation of facts with bound vectors only. First we provide a condition (Theorem 1) that guarantees that a program (that may be the result of magic rewriting) does not derive facts with unbound vectors. Then we describe a class of programs that after being magic rewritten satisfy the condition of Theorem 1.

THEOREM 1 *A program will always produce facts with bound vector variables if in all rules "_H(_V) : − tail" tail has a non-metapredicate subgoal that refers to _V, or in general _V can be assigned a binding if all non-metapredicate subgoals in tail are bound.*

Intuitively, after we magic-rewrite a program it will keep deriving facts with unbound vectors only if a nonterminal of the initial program derives uninstantiated vectors and in the rules that is used it does not share variables with predicates or nonterminals s that bind their arguments (otherwise, the magic predicate will force the the rules that produce uninstantiated vectors to focus on bindings of s.) For example, description (D6) does not derive uninstantiated vectors because the nonterminal _Cond, that may derive uninstantiated variables, shares variables with $Table(_A).

Nevertheless magic sets rewriting does not ensure that derived facts have bound vectors. Below we provide a formal criterion for deciding whether after we magic rewrite a program its bottom-up evaluation will derive facts that have bound vectors only. We believe that all reasonable descriptions satisfy the described criterion. First we state a few definitions needed for the formalization of our criterion.

Definition. Target predicate A predicate that appears in some subgoal of the target query.

Definition. Target subgoal A subgoal that uses a target predicate.

Target subgoals always instantiate their arguments using frozen constants. The following definitions capture how arguments of subgoal s are instantiated by other subgoals thereby allowing magic-sets to restrict the firing of rules defining s.

Definition. Grounded Subgoal in a Rule R A target subgoal is grounded. A nonterminal subgoal is grounded as defined by Definition 4.1. A metapredicate subgoal s is grounded if s can be evaluated using the bindings of those arguments that appear in grounded subgoals of R.

Definition. Grounded Rule A rule is grounded if every vector variable in the rule appears in some grounded subgoal. The rule is said to *depend* on the predicates of the grounded subgoals.

Definition. Grounded nonterminal A nonterminal _N is grounded if each rule defining _N is grounded. For its grounding, _N depends on a nonterminal _M if some rule defining _N depends on _M.

Grounded rules derive instantiated facts and only instantiated facts are derived for grounded nonterminals. We consider only those descriptions where all nonterminals are grounded. For such descriptions magic-sets rewriting always produces production rules that can be evaluated bottom-up without deriving facts with vector variables.

THEOREM 2 *If each nonterminal in a description D is grounded then a bottom-up evaluation of magic-sets rewritten D produces no fact that has vector variables.*

Descriptions that satisfy the above condition are considered *valid*.

THEOREM 3 *Nonterminals of a valid program can be completely ordered such that nonterminal _N in position i depends for its groundings only on nonterminal in positions* $1 \ldots i - 1$.

The following algorithm derives CSQs given a target query and description. Notice that the following algorithm uses the Algorithm 2 of Figure 3, which may be skipped in a first reading. Understanding fully Algorithm 2 requires reading first the passing bindings join techniques discussed in Section 5.

Algorithm 1
Input: Target query Q and Description D
Output: A set of CSQs $s_i, i = 1, \ldots, n$
Method:
    Check if the description D is valid
    Reorder each template R in D such that
        All predicate subgoals occur in the front of the rule
        A nonterminal _N appears after _M if _N depends on _M for grounding.
        Metapredicates appear at the end of the rule
    Rewrite D using Magic-sets
    Evaluate bottom-up the rewritten description D as per Algorithm 2 of Figure 3

4.2. Retaining Only "Representative" CSQs

A large number of unneeded CSQs are generated by templates that use vectors and the _subset metapredicate. For example, template (QT12.1) describes for a particular _A all CSQs that have in their head any subset of variables in _A. It is not necessary to generate all possible CSQs. Instead, for all CSQs that are derived from the same expansion e, of some template t, where e has the form

answer(_V) :- ⟨*predicate and metapredicate list*⟩, _subset(_V,_W)

and _V does not appear in the ⟨*predicate and metapredicate list*⟩ we generate only the *representative* CSQ that is derived by mapping _V to the same variable list as _W.[5] All *represented* CSQs, *i.e.*, CSQs that are derived from e by mapping _V to a proper subset of _W are not generated. For example, the representative CSQ (Q15) and the represented CSQ (Q18) both are derived from the expansion (E22) of template (QT12.1).

```
(E22) answer(_R)  :- $Table(_A),
      _in($Position,X,_A), substring(X,'B'),
      _subset(_R,_A)
```

The CSQ discovery module generates only (Q15) and not (Q18) because (Q15) has fewer attributes than (Q18) and is derived by by mapping the vector _R to the same vector with _A, i.e., to [F1,L1,D,O1,M1]. Representative CSQs often retain unneeded attributes and consequently *Representative plans*, i.e., plans containing representative CSQs, retrieve unneeded attributes. The unneeded attributes are projected out by the plan refinement module.

THEOREM 4 *Retaining only representative CSQs does not lose any plan, i.e., if there is an algebraically optimal plan p_s that involves a represented query s then p_s will be discovered by the CBR.*
Proof: The proof is based on the fact that for every plan p_s there is a corresponding representative plan p_r derived by replacing all CSQs of p_s with their representatives. For simplicity, let us assume that p_s involves only one represented CSQ (that is the CSQ s.) If r is the CSQ that represents s then the plan construction module will output a plan p_r, identical to p_s modulo that it uses r instead of s. The plan refinement module potentially removes some subgoals from the set of consumed subgoals of r. The remaining set of consumed subgoals is either identical to the consumed set of s or it is smaller. If it is identical, then by replacing the necessary variables of r with the necessary variables of the set we get the query with the smaller head that consumes the same set with s. Given that s is algebraically optimal, s is the query we found by reforming r. If the reduced set of consumed subgoals of r is smaller than the set of subgoals consumed by s, then r will have fewer exported variables than s and hence s is not algebraically optimal (it has same body with r but more variables.)

Evaluation: Retaining only a representative CSQ of head arity a eliminates $2^a - 1$ represented CSQs thus eliminating an exponential factor from the execution time and from the size of the output of the CSQ discovery module. Still, one might ask why the CSQ discovery phase does not remove the variables that can be projected out. The reason is that the "projection" step is better done after plans are formed because at that time information is available about the other CSQs in the plan and the way they interact (see Section 6). Thus, though postponing projection pushes part of the complexity to a later stage, it eliminates some complexity altogether. The eliminated complexity corresponds to those represented CSQs that in the end do not participate in any plan because they retain too few variables.

4.3. Pruning Non-Maximal CSQs

Further efficiency can be gained by eliminating any CSQ Q that has fewer subgoals than some other CSQ Q' because Q checks fewer conditions than Q'. A CSQ is maximal if there is no CSQ with more subgoals and the same set of exported variables, modulo variable renaming. We formalize maximality in terms of subsumption [24]:

Definition. Maximal CSQs A CSQ s_m is a *maximal CSQ* if there is no other CSQ s that is subsumed by s_m.

Algorithm 2
    Input: A set of production rules of description D.
            Set of frozen facts F corresponding to the target query Q.
    Output: All facts derivable from applying D to F
    Method:
            Initialize to {} the set (A) of frozen constants
                                                available in answer derived facts.
            Initialize to {} the set (NA) of frozen constants newly
                                                available in answer derived facts.
        Repeat until no new facts are derived
            For each rule r in the description
                Apply rule r to base facts as per Algorithm 3 of Figure 4
                        % Eliminate facts that use bindings not yet available
                Eliminate facts s where $\mathcal{B}_s$ has a frozen constant x where $x \notin A$
                        % Eliminate facts that do not use at least one new binding
                Eliminate facts s where $\mathcal{B}_s$ has frozen constant x where $x \in NA$
                        % Update the sets of available and newly available frozen constants
                Add the set of frozen constants in the heads of
                                                the new derived facts to (NA)
                Remove from (NA) those frozen constants also present in (A)
                Add (NA) to (A)

Figure 3. Bottom-Up Evaluation of a Description

Evaluation: In general, the CSQ discovery module generates only *maximal* CSQs and prunes all others. This pruning technique is particularly effective when the CSQs contain a large number of conditions. For example, assume that g conditions are applied to the variables of a predicate. Consequently, there are $2^g - 1$ CSQs where each one of them contains a different proper subset of the conditions. By keeping "maximal CSQs only" we eliminate an exponential factor of 2^g from the output size of the CSQ discovery module.

THEOREM 5 *Pruning non-maximal CSQs does not lose any algebraically optimal plan.*
Proof: For every plan p_s involving a non-maximal CSQ s there is also a plan p_m that involves the corresponding maximal CSQ s_m such that p_m pushes more selections and/or joins to the wrapper than p_s, since s_m by definition involves more selections and/or joins than s.

5. Plan Construction

In this section we present the plan construction module (see Figure 2.) In order to generate a (representative) plan we have to select a subset S of the CSQs that provides all the

Algorithm 3
    Input: Production rule R
        A set of frozen base facts
        A set of derived facts s associated with annotations:
            C_s, the set of frozen facts of the initial
                                      database that have been used for deriving s
            B_s, the set of variables needed by the subgoals
                                      that correspond to the facts of C_s
    Output: Derived facts + annotations obtained by firing R
                                    using frozen and derived base facts.
    Method:
        % Each alternate unification may yield many facts.
        Unify each subgoal in the body of R with a base fact deriving fact n
        For each _equal subgoals s
            if s equates a frozen variable x to itself then s can be ignored
            if s equates two different frozen variables
                then the whole unification fails
            if s equates a frozen constant c and a place holder
                then add c to annotation B_n
        For each _**subset** subgoal $s =$ _**subset**(Sub, Super)
            if Sub and Super are different vector variables,
                then unification fails
            if Sub and Super are instantiated vectors
                      and Sub is not a subset of Super then fail.
            if only Super is instantiated then equate Sub to the same vector.
            In all other cases unification fails
         For each _**in** subgoal $s =$ _**in**(Pos, Ele, Vector)
            if Pos, Ele, Vector or Ele, Vector are instantiated
                evaluate subgoal to true/false
            if Pos, Vector are instantiated
                then assign Ele the appropriate value
            if Vector is instantiated
                then assign Pos, Ele all possible values
            In all other cases unification fails
         For each non-meta subgoal s
            Add C_s to C_n; Add B_s to B_n
        % Eliminate non-maximal facts
        If derived fact n has smaller annotation C_n, larger B_n,
                    and same set of exported variables with some existing fact n'
            then do not add n to set of derived facts.

Figure 4. Algorithm for the Evaluation of a Single Rule

information needed by the target query, *i.e.*, (i) the CSQs in S check all the subgoals of the target query, (ii) the results in S can be joined correctly, and (iii) each CSQ in S receives the constants necessary for its evaluation. Section 5.1 addresses (i) with the notion of "subgoal consumption." Section 5.2 checks (ii), *i.e.*, checks join variables. Section 5.3 checks (iii) by ensuring bindings are available. Finally, Section 5.4 summarizes the conditions required for constructing a plan and provides an efficient plan construction algorithm.

5.1. Set of Consumed Subgoals

We associate with each CSQ a set of consumed subgoals that describes the CSQs contribution to a plan. Loosely speaking, a component query consumes a subgoal if it extracts all the required information from that subgoal. A CSQ does not necessarily consume all its subgoals. For example, consider a CSQ s_e that semijoins the emp relation with the dept relation to output each emp tuple that is in some department in relation dept. Even though this CSQ has a subgoal that refers to the dept relation it may not always consume the dept subgoal. In particular, consider a target query Q that requires the names of all employees and the location of their departments. CSQ s_e does not output the location attribute of table dept and thus does not consume the dept subgoal with respect to query Q. We formalize the above intuition by the following definition:

Definition. Set of Consumed Subgoals for a CSQ A set S_s of subgoals of a CSQ s constitutes a *set of consumed subgoals* of s if and only if

1. s exports every distinguished variable of the target query that appears in S_s, and

2. s exports every join variable that appears in S_s and also appears in a subgoal of the target query that is not in S_s.

THEOREM 6 *Each CSQ s has a unique* maximal *set C_s of consumed subgoals that is a superset of every other set of consumed subgoals.*
Proof: s has at least one set of consumed subgoals (trivially, the empty set is a set of consumed subgoals.) and hence it has at least one maximal set of consumed subgoals. Let us assume that there are two maximal sets C_s^1 and C_s^2. Then, their union is also a consumed set since it satisfies both conditions of definition 5.1. Hence, C_s^1 and C_s^2 can not simultaneously be maximal consumed sets.

Intuitively the maximal set describes the "largest" contribution that a CSQ may have in a plan. The following algorithm states how to compute the set of maximal consumed subgoals of a CSQ. We annotate every CSQ s with its set of maximal consumed subgoals, C_s.

Algorithm 4
   Input: CSQ s and target query Q
   Output: CSQ s with computed annotation C_s
   Method:
       Insert in C_s all subgoals of s

> Remove from C_s subgoals that have a
> distinguished attribute of Q not exported by s
> Repeat until size of C_s is unchanged
>> Remove from C_s subgoals that:
>>> Join on variable V with subgoal g
>>> of Q where g is not in C_s, and
>>> Join variable V is not exported by s
> Discard CSQ s if C_s is empty.

This algorithm is polynomial in the number of the subgoals and variables of the CSQ. Also, the algorithm discards all CSQs that are not *relevant* to the target query:

Definition. Relevant CSQ A CSQ s is called *relevant* if C_s is non-empty.

Intuitively, irrelevant CSQs are pruned out because in most cases they do not contribute to a plan, since they do not consume any subgoal. Note, we decide the relevance of a CSQ "locally," *i.e.*, without considering other CSQs that it may have to join with. By pruning non-relevant CSQs we can build an efficient plan construction algorithm that in most cases (Section 5.2) produces each plan in time polynomial in the number of CSQs produced by the CSQ discovery module. However, there are scenarios where the relevance criteria may erroneously prune out a CSQ that could be part of a plan. The following example provides such a scenario.

Example: Consider a variation of the wrapper file-wrap (D6) where the supported queries that accept substring conditions may output only the first and last name, e.g., (Q24). There is also a supported query – (Q25) – that returns the whole emp table. The target query (Q23), that requests the full information of employees in the "database" department can be answered by the plan (P26).

> (Q23) answer(F,L,D,O,M) :- emp(F,L,D,O,M), substring(O,'database')
> (Q24) answer$_{24}$(F,L) :- emp(F,L,D,O,M), substring(O,'database ')
> (Q25) answer$_{25}$(F,L,D,O,M) :- emp(F,L,D,O,M)
> (P26) answer (F,L,D,O,M) :- answer$_{24}$(F,L), answer$_{25}$(F,L,D,O,M)

CBR will not find the plan (P26) because the CSQ (Q25) does not consume any subgoal because it does not export the distinguished variables D, O, and M. Intuitively, (Q25) does not contribute subgoals but it contributes variables. □

We may avoid the loss of such plans by not pruning irrelevant CSQs and thus sacrificing the polynomiality of the plan construction algorithm. In this paper we will not consider this option.

5.2. Join Variables Condition

It is not always the case that if the union of consumed subgoals of some CSQs is equal to the set of the target query's subgoals then the CSQs together form a plan. In particular, it is possible that the join of the CSQs may not constitute a plan. For example, consider an online employee database that can be queries for the names of all employees in a given division. The database can also be queried for the names of all employees in a given location. Further, the name of an employee is not uniquely determined by their location and division. The employee database cannot be used to find employees in a given division and in a given location by joining the results of two queries - one on division and the other on location. To see this, consider a query that looks for employees in "CS" in "New York". Joining the results of two independent queries on division and location will incorrectly return as answer a person named "John Smith" if there is a "John Smith" in "CS" in "San Jose" and a different "John Smith" in "Electrical" in "New York".

Intuitively, the problem arises because the two independent queries do not export the information necessary to correctly join their results. We can avoid this problem by checking that CSQs are combined only if they export the join variables necessary for their correct combination. The theorem of Section 5.4 formally describes the conditions on join variables that guarantee the correct combination of CSQs.

5.3. Passing Required Bindings via Nested Loops Joins

The CBR's plans may emulate joins that could not be pushed to the wrapper, with nested loops joins where one CSQ passes join variable bindings to the other. For example, we may compute (Q13) by the following steps: first we execute (Q27); then we collect the department names (*i.e.*, the D bindings) and for each binding d of D, we replace the $D in (Q28) with d and send the instantianted query to the wrapper. We use the notation /$D in the nested loops plan (P29) to denote that (Q28) receives values for the $D placeholder from D *bindings* of the other CSQs – (Q27) in this example.

(Q27) answer_{27}(F0,L0,D,OO):-emp(F0,L0,D,OO,'Y')
(Q28) answer_{28}(F1,L1,O1,M1):-emp(F1,L1,$D,O1,M1)
(P29) answer(F0,L0,O1):-answer_{27}(F0,L0,D,OO),answer_{28}(F1,L1,O1,M1)/$D

The introduction of nested loops and *binding passing* poses the following requirements on the CSQ discovery:

* **CSQ discovery:** A subgoal of a CSQ s may contain placeholders /$⟨var⟩, such as $D, in place of corresponding join variables (D in our example.) Whenever this is the case, we introduce the structure /$⟨var⟩ next to the answer_s that appears in the plan. All the variables of s that appear in such a structure are included in the set $\mathcal{B}_s$, called the *set of bindings needed by* s. For example, $\mathcal{B}_{28} = \{D\}$ and $\mathcal{B}_{27} = \{\}$. CSQ discovery previously did not use bindings information while deriving facts. Thus, the algorithm derives useless CSQs that need bindings not exported by any other CSQ.

  The optimized derivation process uses two sets of attributes and proceeds iteratively. Each iteration derives only those facts that use bindings provided by existing facts. In addition, a fact is derived if it uses at least one binding that was made available only in the very last iteration. Thus, the first iteration derives facts that need no bindings, that is, for which $\mathcal{B}_s$ is empty. The next iteration derives facts that use at least one binding provided by facts derived in iteration one. Thus, the second iteration does not derive any subgoal derived in the first iteration, and so on. The complete algorithm of Figure 3 formalizes this intuition.

The bindings needed by each CSQ of a plan impose order constraints on the plan. For example, the existence of D in $\mathcal{B}_{28}$ requires that a CSQ that exports D is executed before (Q28). It is the responsibility of the plan construction module to ensure that the produced plans satisfy the order constraints.

Evaluation The pruning of CSQs with inappropriate bindings prunes an exponential number of CSQs in the following common scenario: Assume we can put an equality condition on any variable of a subgoal p. Consider a CSQ s that contains p and assume that n variables of p appear in subgoals of the target query that are not contained in s. Then we have to generate all 2^n versions of s that describe different binding patterns. Assuming that no CSQ may provide any of the n variables it is only one (out the 2^n) CSQs useful.

5.4. A Plan Construction Algorithm

In this section we summarize the conditions that are sufficient for construction of a plan. Then, we present an efficient algorithm that finds plans that satisfy the theorem's conditions. Finally, we evaluate the algorithm's performance.

THEOREM 7 *Given CSQs $s_i, i = 1, \ldots, n$ with corresponding heads*
$\text{answer}_i(V_1^i, \ldots, V_{v_i}^i)$, *sets of maximal consumed subgoals $\mathcal{C}_i$ and sets of needed bindings $\mathcal{B}_i$, the plan*

$$\text{answer}(V_1, \ldots, V_m) : -\text{answer}_1(V_1^1, \ldots, V_{v_1}^1), \ldots, \text{answer}_n(V_1^n, \ldots, V_{v_n}^n)$$

is correct if

- **consumed sets condition:** *The union of maximal consumed sets $\cup_{i=1,\ldots,n} \mathcal{C}_i$ is equal to the target query's subgoal set.*

- **join variables condition:** *If the set of maximal consumed subgoals of CSQ s_i has a join variable V then every CSQ s_j that contains V in its set of maximal consumed subgoals $\mathcal{C}_j$ exports V.*

- **bindings passing condition:** *If $V \in \mathcal{B}_i$ then there must be a CSQ $s_j, j < i$ that exports V.*

Proof: We will show that the plan computes the same result with the target query when they are evaluated over the same database.

Let us first consider plans that do not contain nested loops joins. We will show the equivalence of the plan and the target query by showing that there is a mapping from the plan to the target query and vice versa. Note, we consider queries and descriptions in normal form. Let us assume that the target query has the form

$$\text{answer}(H_1, \ldots, H_h) : -g_1(V_1^1, \ldots, V_{v_1}^1), \ldots, g_m(V_1^m, \ldots, V_{v_m}^m) \tag{1}$$

every variable of the head appears in the tail. The plan has the form

$$\text{answer}(H_1, \ldots, H_h) : -\text{answer}_1(A_1^1, \ldots, A_{a_1}^1), \ldots, \text{answer}_l(A_1^n, \ldots, A_{a_n}^n) \quad (2)$$

where every variable of the head appears in the tail. The ith CSQ has the form

$$\text{answer}_i(A_1^i, \ldots, A_{a_i}^i) : -$$
$$g_{\theta(i,1)}(V_1^{\theta(i,1)}, \ldots, V_{v_{\theta(i,1)}}^{\theta(i,1)}), \ldots, g_{\theta(i,m_i)}(V_{m_i}^{\theta(i,m_i)}, \ldots, V_{v_{\theta(i,m_i)}}^{\theta(i,m_i)}) \quad (3)$$

where the function θ maps subgoals of the CSQs to subgoals of the original target query 1.
Using 3 we can rewrite 2 as follows:

$$\text{answer}(H_1, \ldots, H_n) : -$$
$$g_{\theta(1,1)}(X_1^{\theta(1,1)}, \ldots, X_{v_{\theta(1,1)}}^{\theta(1,1)}), \ldots, g_{\theta(1,m_1)}(X_{m_1}^{\theta(1,m_1)}, \ldots, X_{v_{\theta(1,m_1)}}^{\theta(1,m_1)}), \quad (4)$$
$$g_{\theta(n,1)}(X_1^{\theta(n,1)}, \ldots, X_{v_{\theta(n,1)}}^{\theta(n,1)}), \ldots, g_{\theta(n,m_n)}(X_{m_n}^{\theta(n,m_n)}, \ldots, X_{v_{\theta(n,m_n)}}^{\theta(n,m_n)})$$

where the variables that appear in the tail are identical to the ones that appear in the original
CSQ if they appear in the CSQ's head. Otherwise, we rename the original variables of the
CSQ so that they are not identical to the variables introduced by any other CSQ. Formally,

$$X_k^{\theta(i,j)} = \{ \begin{array}{l} V_k^{\theta(i,j)}, \textit{if } V_k^{\theta(i,j)} \in \{A_1^i, \ldots, A_{a_i}^i\} \\ N_k^{\theta(i,j)}, \textit{if } V_k^{\theta(i,j)} \notin \{A_1^i, \ldots, A_{a_i}^i\} \end{array} \quad (5)$$

If $V_k^{\theta(i,j)}$ is identical to $V_{k'}^{\theta(i,j')}$ then $N_k^{\theta(i,j)}$ is identical to $N_{k'}^{\theta(i,j')}$.

Now we will show that there is a mapping from the target query 1 to the plan 4 and vice
versa. We map the plan 4 to the query 1 by mapping the variables $X_k^{\theta(i,j)}$ that are equivalent
to some $N_k^{\theta(i,j)}$ to $V_k^{\theta(i,j)}$. The heads are identical so we do not have to do anything to
establish a mapping.

Then, we map the query 1 to the plan 4. Essentially, we map the subgoals of the target
query that correspond to the consumed set of a CSQ to the subgoals of the CSQ. It is not
obvious that this can happen because the sets of consumed subgoals of the CSQs share
variables.

First we map the subgoals of the target query that correspond to C_1 to the the tail of the
first CSQ, then we map the subgoals of the target query that correspond to $C_2 - C_1$ to to
subgoals of the second CSQ and so on. Let us assume, without loss of the generality, that
$C_i - C_{i-1} - \ldots - C_1$ consists of

$$g_j(V_1^j, \ldots, V_{v_j}^j), j = 1, \ldots, c_i$$

For every $g_j(V_1^j, \ldots, V_{v_j}^j)$ there is a j' such that $\theta(i, j') = j$ (because of the consumed
sets condition). We map $g_j(V_1^j, \ldots, V_{v_j}^j)$ to $g_j(X_1^j, \ldots, X_{v_j}^j)$. The mapping is possible
because:

- if V_k^j has appeared either in the target query head or in $C_{i'}$ where $i' < i$ then because of
  the definition of set of consumed subgoals and because of the join variables condition
  it is guaranteed that V_k^j appears in the head of CSQ i, i.e., $V_k^j \in \{A_1^i, \ldots, A_{a_i}^i\}$, and it
  also appears in the head of CSQ i', i.e., $V_k^j \in \{A_1^{i'}, \ldots, A_{a_{i'}}^{i'}\}$. Hence, X_k^j is identical
  to V_k^j and V_k^j has been earlier mapped to itself.

- otherwise, we map V_k^j to X_k^j.

Plans involving nested loops can (conceptually) be reduced to corresponding plans with local joins by moving the variables of the sets $\mathcal{B}$ in the head of the CSQ if they do not appear already in the head. Then the equivalence of the plan and the target query is obvious, provided that we can execute the plan. The bindings passing condition guarantees that we can execute the plan.

The plan construction algorithm of Figure 5 is based on Theorem 7. The algorithm takes as input a set of CSQs derived by the CSQ discovery process described later, and the target query Q. At each step the algorithm selects a CSQ s that consumes at least one subgoal that has not been consumed by any CSQ s' considered so far and for which all variables of $\mathcal{B}_s$ have been exported by at least one s'. Assuming that the algorithm is given m CSQs (by the CSQ discovery module) it can construct a set that satisfies the consumed sets and the bindings passing conditions in time polynomial in m. Nevertheless, if the join variables condition does not hold the algorithm takes time exponential in m because we may have to create exponentially many sets until we find one that satisfies the join variables condition. However, the join variables condition evaluates to true for most wrappers we find in practice (see following discussion) and thus we usually construct a plan in time polynomial in m.

For every plan p there may be plans p' that are identical to p modulo a permutation of the CSQs of p. In the worst case there are $n_p!$ permutations, where n_p is the number of CSQs in p. Since it is useless to generate permutations of the same plan, The algorithm creates a total order $\prec$ of the input CSQs and generates plans by considering CSQ s_1 before CSQ s_2 only if $s_1 \prec s_2$, i.e., the CSQs are considered in order by $\prec$. Note, a query s_2 must always be considered after a query s_1 if s_1 provides bindings for s_2. Hence, $\prec$ must respect the partial order $\overset{\prec}{b}$ where $s_1 \overset{\prec}{b} s_2$ if s_1 provides bindings to s_2.

The plan construction algorithm first sorts the input CSQs in a total order that respects the PO $\overset{b}{\prec}$. Then it proceeds by picking CSQs and testing the conditions of Theorem 7 until it consumes all subgoals of the target query. The algorithm capitalizes on the assumption that in most practical cases every CSQ consumes at least one subgoal and the join variables condition holds. In this case, one plan is developed in time polynomial in the number of input CSQs. The following lemma describes an important case where the join variables condition always holds.

LEMMA 1 *The join variables condition holds for any set of CSQs such that*

1. *no two CSQs of the set have intersecting sets of maximal consumed subgoals, or*

2. *if two CSQs contain the subgoal $g(V_1, \ldots, V_m)$ in their sets of maximal consumed subgoals then they both export variables $V_1, \ldots, V_m$.*

Condition (1) of Lemma 1 holds for typical wrappers of bibliographic information systems and lookup services (wrappers that have the structure of (D12)), relational databases and object oriented databases – wrapped in a relational model. In such systems it is typical that if two CSQs have common subgoals then they can be combined to form a single CSQ. Thus, we end up with a set of maximal CSQs that have non-intersecting consumed sets. Condition (2) further relaxes the condition (1). Condition (2) holds for all wrappers that can

Algorithm 5
   Input: A set of CSQs $\{s_1, \ldots, s_m\}$
          A target query Q
   Output: A set of plans that satisfy Theorem 7
           and no two plans contain exactly the same CSQs

   Method: Invoke procedure $sort(\{s_1, \ldots, s_m\}, L_0)$ % sort input in L_0 using $\overset{b}{\prec}$
           Invoke procedure $plan(L_0, \{\})$

Procedure $plan(L, P)$
                                                % P is list of CSQs that form part of a plan
                              % L is a sorted list of CSQs that are considered for generating P
                                    % $sub(P)$ refers to the union of the consumed sets
                                              C_i of the CSQs s_i of the set P
   If $sub(P)$ is equal to the set of subgoals of the target query Q
      output plan "$\langle Q\ head \rangle$:- $\langle s_1\ head \rangle \ldots \langle s_n\ head \rangle$"
         where $P = [s_1, \ldots, s_n]$
   Else
      Scan L from the start to the end until we find a CSQ s such that
                                        % s consumes at least one more subgoal
         C_s has at least one subgoal not in $sub(P)$
                                              % Bindings needed by s are available
         All variables V of $\mathcal{B}_s$ are either exported by at least one CSQ in P
            or there is a predicate _**equal**(V, W)
            and W is exported by at least one CSQ in P
      If no s is found return   % no plan can be derived
      Else
                              % Define for s $JV(s)$ the set of join variables
                              %corresponding to joins not pushed down
         For each variable V of each consumed subgoal of s
            If _**equal**(V, W) occurs in Q and W is in a subgoal not consumed by s
               Add V to $JV(s)$
                                        % check join variables condition of Theorem 7
         For each variable V in $JV(s)$ such that _**equal**(V,W) occurs in Q
            Ensure W is exported by each CSQ in P
                     that has a consumed subgoal using W.
         For each CSQ $p \in P$
            For each variable V in $JV(p)$
                     such that _**equal**(V,W) occurs in Q and W appears in s
               Ensure W is exported by s
         Invoke $plan(L', P')$,
                  where L' is the suffix of L that follows s and $P' = concatenate(P, [s])$
         Invoke $plan(L', P)$ %find all plans that do not have s

Figure 5. The Plan Construction Algorithm

export all variables that appear in a CSQ. The two conditions of Lemma 1 cover essentially any wrapper of practical importance.

6. Plan Refinement

The plan refinement module filters and refines constructed plans in two ways. First, it eliminates plans that are not algebraically optimal. The fact that CSQs of the representative plans have the maximum number of selections and joins and that plan refinement pushes the maximum number of projections down is not enough to guarantee that the plans produced are algebraically optimal. For example, assume that CSQs s_1 and s_2 are interchangeable in all plans, and the set of subgoals of s_1 is a superset of the set of subgoals of s_2 and s_1 exports a subset of the variables exported by s_2. The plans in which s_2 participates are algebraically worse than the corresponding plans with s_1. Nevertheless, they are produced by the plan construction module because s_1 and s_2 may both be maximal, and do not represent each other because they are produced by different template expansions. Plan refinement must therefore eliminate plans that include s_2.

Plan refinement must also project out unnecessary variables from representative CSQs. Intuitively, the *necessary* variables of a representative CSQ are those variables that allow the consumed set of the CSQ to "interface" with the consumed sets of other CSQs in the plan. We formalize this notion and its significance by the following definition (note, the definition is not restricted to maximal consumed sets):

Definition. Necessary Variables of a Set of Consumed Subgoals: A variable V is a necessary variable of the consumed subgoals set S_s of some CSQ s if, by not exporting V, S_s is no longer a consumed set.

The set of necessary variables is easily computed: Given a set of consumed subgoals S, a variable V of S is a necessary variable if it is a distinguished variable, or if it is a join variable that appears in at least one subgoal that is not in S.

The complete plan refinement algorithm appears in Figure 6. Its main complication is due to the fact that unnecessary variables cannot always be projected out when the maximal consumed sets of the CSQs intersect. For example, consider a wrapper that exports predicates emp and substring. Every supported query has exactly one emp subgoal, at most one substring subgoal, and may export any subset of the emp variables. The target query (Q30) can be computed by plan (P33).

(Q30) answer(F,L):-emp(F,L,D,O,M),substring(D,'data'),substring(O,'B')
(Q31) answer$_{31}$(F,L,D,O,M) :- emp(F,L,D,O,M), substring(D,'data')
(Q32) answer$_{32}$(F,L,D,O,M) :- emp(F,L,D,O,M), substring(O,'B')
(P33) answer(F,L) :- answer$_{31}$(F,L,D,O,M), answer$_{32}$(F,L,D,O,M)

Having both queries export all the variables is useless. An obvious optimization is to replace (Q32) with (Q34), which exports only the distinguished variables F and L and the join variable D.

(Q34) answer$_{34}$(F,L,D) :- emp(F,L,D,O,M), substring(O,'B')

Algorithm 6
Input: Plan P involving representative CSQ s.
Output: One ormore plans with s replaced by a CSQ
                    with fewer distinguished attributes
Method:
    % Prune the set of maximal consumed subgoals of s
    For each subset M of the set of maximal consumed subgoals of s
        Replace annotation C_s by M
        % Check that the resulting plan is legal
        % sub(P) refers to the union of the maximal consumed sets of plan P
        If $sub(P)$ contains all subgoals of Q then proceed else discard M
        % consumes all subgoals
        Compute set of necessary variables V of s as per Definition 6.
        If V is not a subset of the set of variables exported by s
            discard M
        Else replace the set of exported variables of s by V
            to construct a new plan P'
        % Check if P' is an algebraically optimal plan and discard plans
        % that are algebraically worse than P'
        for every discovered plan P''
            if P' is algebraically worse (see Definition) than P''
                discard P' and exit loop
            else if P'' is algebraically worse than P'
                discard P''

Figure 6. The Plan Refinement Algorithm

Indeed, variables F, L and D are the only *necessary* variables of the maximal consumed subgoals set {emp(F,L,D,O,M), substring(O,'B')}.

However, reducing the exported variables of each representative query to the necessary variables of its maximal consumed set may result in an incorrect plan. For example, replacing CSQ (Q31) with CSQ (Q35) we construct the erroneous plan (P36). (P36) violates the join variables condition.

    (Q35) answer$_{35}$(F,L,O) :- emp(F,L,D,O,M), substring(D,'data')
    (P36) answer(F,L) :- answer$_{34}$(F,L,D), answer$_{35}$(F,L,O)

The problem arises because the maximal consumed sets of (Q31) and (Q32) intersect. It can be solved as follows: Since CSQ (Q34) consumes the subgoals emp(F,L,D,O,M) and substring(O,'B') we can modify the exported variables of the representative CSQ (Q31) so that it consumes only the subgoal
substring(D,'data'). Thus, we can replace the representative CSQ (Q31) with the

CSQ (Q37) that exports only the necessary variables of the set {substring(D,'data')}, *i.e.*, D. Consequently, we can construct the plan (P38).

(Q37) answer$_{37}$(D) :- emp(F,L,D,O,M), substring(D,'data')
(P38) answer(F,L) :- answer$_{34}$(F,L,D), answer$_{37}$(D)

Symmetrically, we may assume that (Q31) consumes emp(F,L,D,O,M) and substring(D,'data') in which case (Q32) consumes only substring(O, 'B') and hence we can produce the plan (P40).

(Q39) answer$_{39}$(O) :- emp(F,L,D,O,M), substring(O,'B')
(P40) answer(F,L) :- answer$_{35}$(F,L,O), answer$_{39}$(O)

Intuitively, the plans (P38) and (P40) correspond to two different partitions of the target query's subgoals among the sets of consumed subgoals the two representative CSQs. In general, given a representative plan, we may produce all plans that implement projections by partitioning the target query subgoals among the representative CSQs. Thus, subgoals that are in the consumed sets of more than one representative query are "assigned" to only one representative query. Then, we calculate the necessary variables for the "reduced" consumed sets of the representative queries.

For ease of explanation we describe an algorithm (see Figure 6) to add projections to a plan with one representative CSQ. The algorithm works also for plans with multiple representative CSQs.

Evaluation The Plan Refinement Algorithm is exponential in the size of C_s. However, it can be optimized by observing the following: If some subgoal in the maximal consumed set of s is not in the maximal consumed set of any other CSQ in plan P, then this subgoal necessarily has to be present in all non-discarded subsets M. Thus, options are generated only by subgoals consumed by multiple CSQs. Thus, the algorithm becomes exponential in the size of the largest intersection of the consumed sets of the representative CSQs.

7. Combining Cost-Based Optimization with Capabilities-Based Rewriting

The previous sections described a capabilities-based rewriter that produces all algebraically optimal plans. Then, a cost-based optimizer estimates the cost of each algebraically optimal plan and selects the absolutely optimal one. However, separating cost optimization and capabilities-based rewriting may result in a huge number (exponential in the number of query subgoals and join variables) of algebraically optimal plans. For sufficiently large queries it may be prohibitively expensive to generate and evaluate all algebraically optimal plans. In this section we solve this problem by incorporating cost optimization and *pruning* into the plan construction phase. The solution follows the same techniques with the well-known System R optimizer [20] and - in accordance with System R - does not compromise in practice the completeness of the optimization (i.e., the optimal plan is discovered) but the running time may still be exponential.

The intuition behind pruning is that we do not want to keep track of all possible (sub)plans to execute and join a subset S of subgoals. We may select the most efficient subplan and use

(Q42) $\text{answer}_{42}(X, Y) : -p(X, Y)$
(Q43) $\text{answer}_{43}(X) : -p(X, \$Y)$
(Q44) $\text{answer}_{44}(Y) : -p(\$X, Y)$
(Q45) $\text{answer}_{45}() : -p(\$X, \$Y)$
(Q46) $\text{answer}_{46}(Y, Z) : -q(Y, Z)$
(Q47) $\text{answer}_{47}(Y) : -q(Y, \$Z)$
(Q48) $\text{answer}_{48}(Z) : -q(\$Y, Z)$
(Q49) $\text{answer}_{49}() : -q(\$Y, \$Z)$
(Q50) $\text{answer}_{50}(Z, W) : -r(Z, W)$
(Q51) $\text{answer}_{51}(Z) : -r(Z, \$W)$
(Q52) $\text{answer}_{52}(W) : -r(\$Z, W)$
(Q53) $\text{answer}_{53}() : -r(\$Z, \$W)$

Figure 7. CSQs for query (Q41)

(Q54) $\text{answer}(X, Y, Z, W) : -\text{answer}_{42}(X, Y), \text{answer}_{46}(Y, Z), \text{answer}_{50}(Z, W)$
(Q55) $\text{answer}(X, Y, Z, W) : -\text{answer}_{42}(X, Y), \text{answer}_{46}(Y, Z), \text{answer}_{52}(W)/\$Z$
(Q56) $\text{answer}(X, Y, Z, W) : -\text{answer}_{42}(X, Y), \text{answer}_{48}(Z)/\$Y, \text{answer}_{50}(Z, W)$
(Q57) $\text{answer}(X, Y, Z, W) : -\text{answer}_{42}(X, Y), \text{answer}_{48}(Z)/\$Y, \text{answer}_{50}(W)/\$Z$

Figure 8. Plans corresponding to the order p, q, r

it whenever we want to join a CSQ s' with the CSQs that compute S. We first provide an example that illustrates the performance problem arising when the CBR and the optimizer operate separately. Then we describe the enhanced CBR algorithm (which includes cost optimization) and we revisit the example.

Example: Consider the following target query

(Q41) $\text{answer}(X, Y, Z, W) :- p(X, Y), q(Y, Z), r(Z, W)$

Assume that the source can answer any query that refers to only one relation and has zero or more equality conditions on the relation attributes. Figure 7 lists the CSQs that will be derived from the plan construction phase. The plan construction algorithm of Figure 5 derives 24 algebraically optimal plans. In particular, for every permutation of p, q, and r there are four possible plans because there are two CSQs that can consume the second subgoal and two CSQs that can consume the third subgoal. Figure 8 lists the plans corresponding to the order p, q, r.

□

If we generalize our scenario to a "chain join" query with n predicates of the form

(Q58) $\texttt{answer}(X_0, X_1 \ldots, X_n, X_{n+1}) : -p_0(X_0, X_1), p_1(X_1, X_2) \ldots p_n(X_n, X_{n+1})$

the number of CSQs is linear in n but the number of plans is exponential in n. Indeed, even for the single permutation $p_0, p_1, \ldots, p_n$ there are 2^n algebraically optimal plans. The plan construction and optimization Algorithm 7 (Figure 9) employs two techniques to reduce the complexity:

1. For every subset S of subgoals it discovers once the optimum subplan to compute the join of the subgoals of S. It will consequently use the optimum plan whenever the CSQs corresponding to these subgoals will be joined with other CSQs.

2. Plans that correspond to cartesian products, i.e., plans where some CSQs do not have any common variables or do not exchange bindings with the rest of the CSQs are not considered.

Algorithm 7 discovers optimal plans for increasingly larger subsets of subgoals. At the end of round i it has discovered the optimal plans for consuming each set with less than $i + 1$ subgoals. It may have also generated some plans that join $i + 1$ or more subgoals because upon trying to consume a set of i subgoals, say, $\{s_1, \ldots, s_i\}$ it may have to use CSQs that consume some additional subgoals such as s_{i+1}.

The following definitions clarify the notion of (sub)plan and "set of subgoals consumed by a plan".

Definition. Plan A plan p of a target query q is a sequence $\langle s_1, \ldots, s_n \rangle$ of CSQs of q such that the bindings passing condition holds, i.e., if $V \in \mathcal{B}_{s_i}$ then there is a CSQ $s_j, j < i$ that exports V.

The "sequence" definition of plan indicates only (1) which CSQs will be used in the plan and (2) what sets of bindings will be received by the CSQs that require bindings. The latter info is implied by the order in which the CSQs appear. We are not concerned with the join order and join policies for the joins that will be done by the mediator. This simplifying assumption is often justified from the predominance of network and source costs.

Definition. Consumed Set of Subgoals A plan $p = \langle s_1, \ldots, s_n \rangle$ *consumes* the set of subgoals $\mathcal{C}_p = \cup_{s_i=1 \ldots n} \mathcal{C}_{s_i}$, i.e. $\mathcal{C}_p$ is the set of subgoals consumed by the CSQs of p.

Notice that we are not concerned with estimating the cost of our plans - though it is an important and difficult problem. Instead, we assume the existence of an appropriate cost estimation function $f(p)$.

Notation: $\langle s_1, \ldots, s_n \rangle \circ s_{n+1} = \langle s_1, \ldots, s_n, s_{n+1} \rangle$.

Example: Let us demonstrate Algorithm 7 in the case of the Example 7. In step $i = 1$ it generates plans consisting of one CSQ (see Figure 10). By the end of step $i = 1$ all plans for singular sets of subgoals have been constructed. However, if there were CSQs consuming more than one subgoal we would also have some sets that consume more than one subgoals.

Algorithm 7

INPUT: (1) a target query q and a set S of CSQs of q
                  (2) a cost function f that estimates the cost of plans

OUTPUT: A plan that computes q (if there is one) and has the least cost

METHOD:

For every CSQ s where $\mathcal{B}_s$ is empty
    insert into $\mathcal{P}$ the plan $\langle s \rangle$
For $i = 2, \ldots, n$ where n is the number of subgoals in q
    For every plan $p = \langle s_1, \ldots, s_m \rangle$ where $\mathcal{C}_p$ has less than i subgoals
        For every CSQ s
            If s consumes at least one subgoal that is not in $\mathcal{C}_p$, and

$$\text{for all } j = 1, \ldots, m : s_j \overset{\prec}{b} s, \text{ and}$$
$$s \text{ exportsat least one variable } V$$
$$\text{that is also exported by a CSQ of } p, \text{ or}$$
$$\mathcal{B}_s \text{ has a variable } V \text{ that is exported by a CSQ of } p$$

                Then create a plan $p' = p \circ s = \langle s_1, \ldots, s_m, s \rangle$
            If there is no plan p'' with $\mathcal{C}_{p''} = \mathcal{C}_{p'}$
                insert p' in $\mathcal{P}$
            Else if there is a plan p'' with $\mathcal{C}_{p''} = \mathcal{C}_{p'}$ and $f(p') < f(p'')$
                delete p'' from $\mathcal{P}$
                insert p' into $\mathcal{P}$
Output the unique plan p (if there is one) where $\mathcal{C}_p$ includes all subgoals of q

Figure 9. Plan Construction Algorithm enhanced with Cost Optimization and Pruning

In step $i = 2$ we pick the best plan for each of the three sets of size one and we "extend" it every time with another CSQ. We use the notation $\langle s_1, \ldots, s_n \rangle \circ s = \langle s_1, \ldots, s_n, s \rangle$ to extend a plan with one more CSQ. Notice that we avoid cartesian products and hence we do not have any plan for the set $\{p, r\}$. Technically, we avoid cartesian products by requiring that the CSQ that will extend a plan shares at least one variable with the plan or takes at least one set of bindings from the plan. Furthermore, we do not generate plans which are mere permutations of each other. For example, we do not extend the optimal plan for consuming q with the CSQ (Q42). Technically, we avoid permutations by producing only sequences that conform to the partial order $\overset{\prec}{b}$ (see Section 5.4).

In step $i = 3$ we pick the optimum plan for each of the two subsets and appropriately extend it. For the sake of the example, let us assume that

$$\langle \text{ans}_{42}(X, Y), \text{ans}_{46}(Y, Z) \rangle$$

is the optimum plan for $\{p, q\}$ and

$$\langle \text{ans}_{50}(Z, W), \text{ans}_{47}(Y)/\$Z \rangle$$

$i = 1$
$\{p\}$
$\langle \text{ans}_{42}(\text{X}, \text{Y}) \rangle$
$\{q\}$
$\langle \text{ans}_{46}(\text{Y}, \text{Z}) \rangle$
$\{r\}$
$\langle \text{ans}_{50}(\text{Z}, \text{W}) \rangle$

$i = 2$
$\{p, q\}$
$\langle \text{ans}_{42}(\text{X}, \text{Y}) \rangle \circ \text{ans}_{46}(\text{Y}, \text{Z}) = \langle \text{ans}_{42}(\text{X}, \text{Y}), \text{ans}_{46}(\text{Y}, \text{Z}) \rangle$
$\langle \text{ans}_{42}(\text{X}, \text{Y}) \rangle \circ \text{ans}_{48}(\text{Z})/\$\text{Y} = \langle \text{ans}_{42}(\text{X}, \text{Y}), \text{ans}_{48}(\text{Z})/\$\text{Y} \rangle$
$\langle \text{ans}_{46}(\text{Y}, \text{Z}) \rangle \circ \text{ans}_{43}(\text{X})/\$\text{Y} = \langle \text{ans}_{46}(\text{Y}, \text{Z}), \text{ans}_{43}(\text{X})/\$\text{Y} \rangle$
$\{q, r\}$
$\langle \text{ans}_{46}(\text{Y}, \text{Z}) \rangle \circ \text{ans}_{50}(\text{Z}, \text{W}) = \langle \text{ans}_{46}(\text{Y}, \text{Z}), \text{ans}_{50}(\text{Z}, \text{W}) \rangle$
$\langle \text{ans}_{46}(\text{Y}, \text{Z}) \rangle \circ \text{ans}_{52}(\text{W})/\$\text{Z} = \langle \text{ans}_{46}(\text{Y}, \text{Z}), \text{ans}_{52}(\text{W})/\$\text{Z} \rangle$
$\langle \text{ans}_{50}(\text{Z}, \text{W}) \rangle \circ \text{ans}_{47}(\text{Y})/\$\text{Z} = \langle \text{ans}_{50}(\text{Z}, \text{W}), \text{ans}_{47}(\text{Y})/\$\text{Z} \rangle$

$i = 3$
$\{p, q, r\}$
$\langle \text{ans}_{42}(\text{X}, \text{Y}), \text{ans}_{46}(\text{Y}, \text{Z}) \rangle \circ \text{ans}_{50}(\text{Z}, \text{W}) = \langle \text{ans}_{42}(\text{X}, \text{Y}), \text{ans}_{46}(\text{Y}, \text{Z}), \text{ans}_{50}(\text{Z}, \text{W}) \rangle$
$\langle \text{ans}_{42}(\text{X}, \text{Y}), \text{ans}_{46}(\text{Y}, \text{Z}) \rangle \circ \text{ans}_{52}(\text{W})/\$\text{Z} = \langle \text{ans}_{42}(\text{X}, \text{Y}), \text{ans}_{46}(\text{Y}, \text{Z}), \text{ans}_{52}(\text{W})/\$\text{Z} \rangle$
$\langle \text{ans}_{50}(\text{Z}, \text{W}), \text{ans}_{47}(\text{Y})/\$\text{Z} \rangle \circ \text{ans}_{43}(\text{X})/\$\text{Y} = \langle \text{ans}_{50}(\text{Z}, \text{W}), \text{ans}_{47}(\text{Y})/\$\text{Z}, \text{ans}_{43}(\text{X})/\$\text{Y} \rangle$
$\langle \text{ans}_{50}(\text{Z}, \text{W}), \text{ans}_{47}(\text{Y})/\$\text{Z} \rangle \circ \text{ans}_{42}(\text{X}, \text{Y}) = \langle \text{ans}_{50}(\text{Z}, \text{W}), \text{ans}_{47}(\text{Y})/\$\text{Z}, \text{ans}_{42}(\text{X}, \text{Y}) \rangle$

Figure 10. Plans constructed and evaluated for the query (Q41)

is the optimal plan for $\{q, r\}$. The optimal plan for $\{p, q\}$ can be extended in two ways; either with $\text{ans}_{50}(\text{Z}, \text{W})$ or with $\text{ans}_{52}(\text{W})/\$\text{Z}$. The optimal plan for for $\{q, r\}$ can be extended with $\text{ans}_{43}(\text{X})/\$\text{Y}$ or with $\text{ans}_{42}(\text{X}, \text{Y})$. □

8. Practical Issues in the Implementation of a Capabilities-Based Rewriter

A capabilities-based rewriter has been implemented for Garlic using Starburst's extensible optimizer [10] as implemented for DB2 [5]. The implementation has enhanced some aspects of capabilities-based rewriting (see the list below) and has simplified algorithms whenever the corresponding functionality loss does not impede the inclusion of target sources. A detailed description of the implementation can be found in [7]. In this section we summarize the most important aspects of the implementation and we compare with the algorithms described in previous section.

- **Capabilities Description Language** In Garlic's implementation of the CBR the capabilities of a wrapper are described via a description of the set of *plans* that can be executed by the wrapper. At a sufficient level of abstraction the plans are trees where the leaves are the source relations and the inner nodes are operators, called *Plan OPerators (POPs)*, such as selection, join, projection, and so on. The role of nonterminals is assumed by the optimizer's *STARs (STrategy Alternative Rules)* which are essentially the production rules of a grammar that generates a possibly infinite number of plans. Describing capabilities using plans – as opposed to queries – facilitated the use of the

Starburst extensible optimizer. However, the use of plans for describing capabilities forces a wrapper writer to understand the meaning and use of plans by the optimizer, complicating the task of writing a description. We plan to work on using a variant of RQDL for the capabilities description.

- **Mediator Capabilities Description** A unique feature of the implementation is that the capabilities of the mediator are also described − as opposed to the algorithms of the previous sections where the mediator can only do selections, projections, and joins. Having an open set of mediator capabilities is important for a system that targets not only conjunctive queries but also aggregates, similarity queries on multimedia data, etc. For example, the implementation introduced a special kind of join that implements the merging of "fuzzy" result sets using an algorithm outlined in [3]. However, we will not further discuss the non-SPJ abilities of the implemented version because the fundamental issues pertaining to capabilities-based rewriting of non-SPJ queries are not yet fully understood. For example, we do not know yet how to characterize the completeness of an algorithm for rewriting aggregates or negations.[6] For the comparison between the CBR algorithms of this paper and the Garlic implementation we assume that we deal with SPJ queries only and that the mediator capabilities include arbitrarily complex plans consisting of selections, projections, and joins.

- **Capabilities-Based Rewriter Operates with Descriptions of Multiple Sources** The target query refers to multiple sources and the description provides all the supported queries of all the sources. It is straightforward to see that the algorithms described in the previous sections are not affected by this feature modulo that the CBR has to keep track of the source that supports a given CSQ in order to issue the right query to the right source.

- **Implementation Architecture** The optimizer operates in three phases. Together, phase 1 and phase 2 do the work of CSQ discovery and plan construction, looking at first single subgoals, and then increasingly larger subsets of subgoals, using rules provided by both mediator and wrappers at each step. We assume that the mediator can retrieve all the variables associated with the tables participating in a plan supported by the wrappers; this assumption reduces plan construction to a search for plans that use all tables appearing in the target query and furthermore it eliminates the need for inserting projections during plan refinement. Finally there is a phase of (essentially minor) refinements and fixes. For example, the attributes are placed in the order requested by the query.

The implementation combines capabilities-based rewriting with cost-based optimization in order to avoid generating all possible algebraically optimal plans (recall, there can be an exponential number of algebraically optimal plans.) In particular, the plan construction phase employs the dynamic programming algorithm of Starburst's optimizer − similar to Algorithm 7 of Figure 9 − for discovering the most efficient supported plan while at the same time it prunes the space of plans. A side effect of the cost-based optimization enhancement is that the prunings for algebraic optimality are not that crucial anymore because they become a special case of the cost-based prunings.

- **Join Variables Condition** The implementation assumes that all variables of the body of a query can be obtained. This assumption is most often valid; it posed no problem to the integration of over 10 different sources, including a relational database, two Web sources, Lotus Notes databases, a chemical structure search engine, text and image content search systems. It greatly simplifies the implementation in two ways. The first one, that we have already discussed, is that it validates the join variables condition (recall, the join variables condition requires that join variables are returned.) Second, the plan refinement step is integrated into plan construction because there is no need to construct plans with too many variables as is done by the plan construction and CSQ discovery of the previous sections.

9. Evaluation

The CBR algorithm employs many techniques to eliminate sources of exponentiality that would otherwise arise in many practical cases. The **evaluation** paragraphs of many sections in this paper describe the benefit we derive from using these techniques. Remember that our assumption that every CSQ consumes at least one subgoal led to a plan construction module that develops a plan in time polynomial to the number of CSQs produced by the CSQ detection module, provided that the join variables condition holds. This is an important result because the join variables condition holds for most wrappers in practice, as argued in Subsection 5.4.

The CBR deals only with Select-Project-Join queries and their corresponding descriptions. It produces algebraically optimal plans involving CSQs, *i.e.*, plans that push the maximum number of selections, projections and joins to the source. However, the CBR is not complete because it misses plans that contain irrelevant CSQs (see Definition 5.1 and the discussion of Section 5.1.) On the other hand, the techniques for eliminating exponentiality preserve completeness, in that we do not miss any plan through applying one of these techniques (see justifications in Sections 4.2, 4.3.)

10. Related Work

Significant results have been developed for the resolution of semantic and schematic discrepancies while integrating heterogeneous information sources. However, most of these systems [19, 8, 1, 6] do not address the problem of different and limited query capabilities in the underlying sources because they assume that those sources are full-fledged databases that can answer any query over their schema.[7] The recent interest in the integration of arbitrary information sources, including databases, file systems, the Web, and many legacy systems, invalidates the assumption that all underlying sources can answer any query over the data they export and forces us to resolve the mismatch between the query capabilities provided by these sources. Only a few systems have addressed this problem.

HERMES [19] proposes a rule language for the specification of mediators in which an explicit set of parameterized calls can be made to the sources. At run-time the parameters are instantiated by specific values and the corresponding calls are made. Thus, HERMES guarantees that all queries sent to the wrappers are supported. Unfortunately, this solution reduces the interface between wrappers and mediators to a very simple form (the particular parameterized calls), and does not fully utilize the sources' query power.

DISCO [22]describes the set of supported queries using context-free grammars. This technique reduces the efficiency of capabilities-based rewriting because it treats queries as "strings."

The Information Manifold [11] develops a query capabilities description that is attached to the schema exported by the wrapper. The description states which and how many conditions may be applied on each attribute. RQDL provides greater expressive power by being able to express schema-independent descriptions and descriptions such as "exactly one condition is allowed."

TSIMMIS suggests an explicit description of the wrapper's query capabilities [14], using the context-free grammar approach of the current paper. (The description is also used for query translation from the common query language to the language of the underlying source.) However, TSIMMIS considers a restricted form of the problem wherein descriptions consider relations of prespecified arities and the mediator can only select or project the results of a single CSQ.

This paper enhances the query capability description language of [14] to describe queries over arbitrary schemas, namely, relations with unspecified arities and names, as well as capabilities such as "selections on the first attribute of any relation." The language also allows specification of required bindings, e.g., a bibliography database that returns "titles of books given author names." We provide algorithms for identifying for a target query Q the algebraically optimal CSQs from the given descriptions. Also, we provide algorithms for generating plans for Q by combining the results of these CSQs using selections, projections, and joins.

The CBR problem is related to the problem of determining how to answer a query using a set of materialized views [13, 9, 18, 17]. However, there are significant differences. These papers consider a specification language that uses SPJ expressions over given relations specifying a finite number of views. They cannot express arbitrary relations, arbitrary arities, binding requirements (with the exception of [18]), or infinitely large queries/views. Also, they do not consider generating plans that require a particular evaluation order due to binding requirements.

[9] shows that rewriting a conjunctive query is in general exponential in the total size of the query and views. [17] shows that if the query is acyclic we can rewrite it in time polynomial to the total size of the query and views. [9, 18] generate necessary and sufficient conditions for when a query can be answered by the available views. By contrast, our algorithms check only sufficient conditions and might miss a plan because of the heuristics used. Our algorithm can be viewed as a generalization of algorithms that decide the subsumption of a datalog query by a datalog program (i.e., the description). [12] proposed Datalog for the description of supported queries. It also suggested an algorithm that essentially finds what we call maximal CSQs. Recently [25] discussed the expressive power of Datalog and the expressive power of an RQDL extension. The most important result was that Datalog cannot express the capabilities of powerful sources. In particular, it is proven that there is no Datalog program that can express the set of all conjunctive queries over a given schema.

It is also proven that RQDL can do so. Furthermore, the extended RQDL is reduced into Datalog with functions.

11. Conclusions and Future Work

In this paper, we presented the Relational Query Description Language, RQDL, which provides powerful features for the description of wrappers' query capabilities. RQDL allows the description of infinite sets of arbitrarily large queries over arbitrary schemas. We also introduced the Capabilities-Based Rewriter, CBR, and presented an algorithm that discovers plans for computing a wrapper's target query using only queries supported by the wrapper. Despite the inherent exponentiality of the problem, the CBR uses optimizations and heuristics to produce plans in reasonable time in most practical situations.

We also described the enhancement of CBR with a cost-based optimizer and we discussed practical issues in the implementation of a capabilities-based rewriting algorithm for Garlic.

Acknowledgments

We are grateful to Mike Carey, Hector Garcia-Molina, Anthony Tomasic, Vasilis Vassalos and Ed Wimmers for many fruitful discussions and comments.

Appendix

(0) ⟨description⟩	::=	(⟨query template⟩|⟨nonterminal template⟩))*
(1) ⟨query template⟩	::=	**answer**(⟨predicate arguments⟩)
		: − ⟨subgoal list⟩
(2) ⟨nonterminal template⟩	::=	⟨nonterminal name⟩ (⟨arguments⟩)
		⟨subgoal list⟩
(3) ⟨subgoal list⟩	::=	⟨subgoal⟩ (, ⟨subgoal⟩)*
(4) ⟨subgoal list⟩	::=	ϵ %subgoal list may be emtpy
(5) ⟨subgoal⟩	::=	⟨predicate⟩ (⟨arguments⟩) %predicate
(6) ⟨subgoal⟩	::=	⟨metapredicate name⟩ (⟨arguments⟩)
(7) ⟨subgoal⟩	::=	⟨nonterminal name⟩ (⟨arguments⟩)
(8) ⟨arguments⟩	::=	⟨vector⟩|⟨variable⟩ (, ⟨variable⟩)*
(9) ⟨predicate name⟩	::=	⟨identifier⟩|⟨placeholder⟩
(10) ⟨metapredicate name⟩	::=	⟨identifier⟩
(11) ⟨nonterminal name⟩	::=	⟨identifier⟩

Figure A.1. Normal-form RQDL syntax

A.1.   Syntax and Semantics of RQDL

In this section we formally present the syntax and semantics of RQDL. We focus on normal-form RQDL. (We may reduce non-normal form descriptions to normal form applying the transformations described in Section 2.4.)

The syntax appears in Figure A.1. Furthermore, we restrict to descriptions where there is a nonterminal template, with matching arity, for every nonterminal that appears in a template. Additionally, for the implementation reasons described in Section 4 we restrict to descriptions where all nonterminals are grounded.

The following definitions formally define the set of queries that is described by a description. First we define the set of expansions of a query template. Then we use the set of *terminal expansions, i.e.*, the set of expansions that do not contain any nonterminal, for defining the set of queries described by terminal expansions and hence described from the description. Note, from a syntactical viewpoint expansions are equivalent to templates.

Definition. Set of expansions $\mathcal{E}_t$ of query template t The set of expansions $\mathcal{E}_t$ contains

1. the template t

2. every expansion e derived by permuting the subgoals of an expansion $g \in \mathcal{E}_t$

3. every expansion e derived by renaming the variables, vectors, and placeholders of an expansion $g \in \mathcal{E}_t$

4. every expansion e of the form

$$\langle answer\ predicate \rangle \ : - \langle N\ definition\ body \rangle, \langle other\ subgoals \rangle$$

such that there is an expansion $g \in \mathcal{E}_t$ that has the form

$$\langle answer\ predicate \rangle \ : - N(\langle arguments \rangle), \langle other\ subgoals \rangle$$

and a nonterminal template of the form

$$N(\langle definition\ arguments \rangle) \ : \ \langle N\ definition\ body \rangle$$

where

(A) the nonterminal template and the expansion e have no common variable,

(B) there is a collection of mappings θ such that $\theta(N(\langle arguments \rangle))$ is identical to $\theta(N(\langle definition\ arguments \rangle))$. We call θ a *unifier*. Definition A.1 formally defines the application of a unifier on an RQDL expression.

Definition. Application of unifier on RQDL expression Given the RQDL expression e, where e may be subgoal, subgoal list, or nonterminal template head, and the unifier θ, $\theta(e)$ is computed by the following steps

1. If θ contains a mapping of the form $\langle placeholder \rangle \mapsto \langle constant \rangle$, or $\langle variable \rangle_1 \mapsto \langle variable \rangle_2$, or $\langle vector \rangle_1 \mapsto \langle vector \rangle_2$ then replace all instances of $\langle placeholder \rangle$, $\langle variable \rangle_1$, and $\langle vector \rangle_2$ with $\langle constant \rangle$, $\langle variable \rangle_2$, or $\langle vector \rangle_2$ respectively.

2. If θ contains a mapping of the form $\langle vector \rangle \mapsto [\langle variable\ list \rangle]$ replace all instances of $\langle vector \rangle$ that appear in metapredicates with $[\langle variable\ list \rangle]$ and all the other instances with $\langle variable\ list \rangle$.

Definition. Set of terminal expansions $\mathcal{T}_t$ of query template t The set of terminal expansions $\mathcal{T}_t$ of a template t consists of all expansions of $\mathcal{E}_t$ that do not contain a nonterminal.

Definition. Set of queries described by query template t The set of queries described by query template t consists of all queries that are obtained by applying the following transformations to an expansion $g \in \mathcal{T}_t$

1. replace every vector with a variable list,

2. replace every placeholder with a constant,

3. remove all metapredicates that evaluate to `true`

If there is at least one metapredicate left then the transformed expansion is *not* a query.

We do not have to include all permutations of subgoals and renamings of variables in the above because $\mathcal{T}_t$ contains all expansions we can derive by subgoals permutations and variable renaming.

Notes

1. In general, there is a one-to-one mapping and no optimization is involved in this translation. All optimization is done at the mediator.
2. We see next that RQDL has nonterminals with parameters. The nonterminals of context-free grammars are a special case with 0 parameters.
3. The "lookup" facility is very similar to a Stanford University facility.
4. We could have used SPJ SQL queries instead of Datalog. Then, we would use a description language that looks like SQL and not Datalog. The same notions, *i.e.*, placeholders, nonterminals, and so on, hold. The CBR algorithm is also the same.
5. In general, the $\langle list\ of\ predicates\ and\ metapredicates \rangle$ may contain metapredicates of the form $\_in(\langle position \rangle, \langle variable_i \rangle), \_V), i = 1, \ldots, m$. In this case, the template describes all CSQs that output a subset of $\_W$ and a superset of $S = \{\langle variable \rangle_1, \ldots, \langle variable \rangle_m\}$. The CSQ discovery module outputs, as usual, the representative CSQ and annotates it with the set S that provides the "minimum" set of variables that represented CSQs must export. In this paper we will not describe any further the extensions needed for the handling of this case.
6. Indeed, there is not a complete algorithm for handling arbitrary SQL queries with negation. This is a consequence of the undecidability, in the general case, of the equivalence of two SQL queries with negation [21].
7. The work in query decomposition in distributed databases has also assumed that all underlying systems are relational and equally able to perform any SQL query.

References

1. R. Ahmed et al. The Pegasus heterogeneous multidatabase system. *IEEE Computer*, 24:19–27, 1991.
2. M.J. Carey et al. Towards heterogeneous multimedia information systems: The Garlic approach. In *Proc. RIDE-DOM Workshop*, pages 124–31, 1995.
3. R. Fagin. Combining fuzzy information from multiple systems. In *Proc. PODS*, 1996.
4. J.C. Franchitti and R. King. Amalgame: a tool for creating interoperating persistent, heterogeneous components. *Advanced Database Systems*, pages 313–36, 1993.
5. P. Gassner, G. Lohman, B. Schiefer, and Y. Wang. Query optimization in the IBM DB2 family. *IEEE Data Engineering Bulletin*, 16:4–18, September 1993.
6. A. Gupta. *Integration of Information Systems: Bridging Heterogeneous Databases*. IEEE Press, 1989.
7. L. Haas, D. Kossman, E. Wimmers, and J. Yang. Optimizing queries across diverse data sources. In *Proc. VLDB*, 1997.
8. J. Hammer and D. McLeod. An approach to resolving semantic heterogeneity in a federation of autonomous, heterogeneous database systems. *Intl Journal of Intelligent and Cooperative information Systems*, 2:51–83, 1993.
9. A. Levy, A. Mendelzon, Y. Sagiv, and D. Srivastava. Answering queries using views. In *Proc. PODS Conf.*, pages 95–104, 1995.
10. G. Lohman. Grammar-like functional rules for representing query optimization alternatives. In *Proc. ACM SIGMOD*, 1988.
11. A. Levy, A. Rajaraman, and J. Ordille. Query processing in the information manifold. In *Proc. VLDB*, 1996.
12. A. Levy, A. Rajaraman, and J. Ullman. Answering queries using limited external processors. In *Proc. PODS*, pages 227–37, 1996.
13. P.A. Larson and H.Z. Yang. Computing queries from derived relations. In *Proc. VLDB Conf.*, pages 259–69, 1985.
14. Y. Papakonstantinou, A. Gupta, H. Garcia-Molina, and J. Ullman. A query translation scheme for the rapid implementation of wrappers. In *Proc. DOOD Conf.*, pages 161–86, 1995.
15. Y. Papakonstantinou, A. Gupta, and L. Haas. Capabilities-based query rewriting in mediator systems. In *Proc. PDIS*, 1996.
16. Y. Papakonstantinou, H. Garcia-Molina, and J. Widom. Object exchange across heterogeneous information sources. In *Proc. ICDE Conf.*, pages 251–60, 1995.
17. Xiaolei Qian. Query folding. In *Proc. ICDE*, pages 48–55, 1996.
18. A. Rajaraman, Y. Sagiv, and J. Ullman. Answering queries using templates with binding patterns. In *Proc. PODS Conf.*, pages 105–112, 1995.
19. V.S. Subrahmanian et al. HERMES: A heterogeneous reasoning and mediator system. http://www.cs.umd.edu/projects/hermes/overview/paper.
20. P. Selinger, M. Astrahan, D. Chamberlin, R. Lorie, and T. Price. Access path selection in a relational database management system. In *Proc. ACM SIGMOD*, 1979.
21. S. Sagiv and M. Yannakakis. Equivalences among relational expressions with the union and difference operators. *JACM*, 27:633–55, 1980.
22. A. Tomasic, L. Raschid, and P. Valduriez. Scaling heterogeneous databases and the design of DISCO. Technical report, INRIA, 1995.
23. J.D. Ullman. *Principles of Database and Knowledge-Base Systems, Vol. I: Classical Database Systems*. Computer Science Press, New York, NY, 1988.
24. J.D. Ullman. *Principles of Database and Knowledge-Base Systems, Vol. II: The New Technologies*. Computer Science Press, New York, NY, 1989.
25. V. Vassalos and Y. Papakonstantinou. Describing and using query capabilities of heterogeneous sources. Available via http://www-cse.ucsd.edu/ yannis/.